THE NEW CONFEDERATION

Five Sovereign Provinces

By
Brian A. Brown

hancock
house

Copyright © 1977 Brian A. Brown
ISBN 0-88839-001-7

Cataloging in Publication Data

Brown, Brian A., 1942-
The New Confederation

Includes index.
ISBN 0-88839-001-7

1. Canada-Politics and government-
1963- * 2. Federal government-Canada.
I. Title
JL 65-1977.B76   320.4'71   C77-002131-X

Published by:

Hancock House Publishers Ltd.
3215 Island View Road
SAANICHTON, B.C. V0S 1M0

Hancock House Publishers Inc.
12008 1st Avenue South
SEATTLE, WA. 98168

To Don and Shirley

Brian A. Brown

PREFACE

In the preface to **Separatism** I indicated that I would be writing in a highly personal style. I suggested that for me to write about Canada is like saying a prayer or composing a love letter, and that to be meaningful such things must be personal. The reaction to that book has encouraged me to believe that such a style is popular even if it breaks the conventions of English Literature.

The pressures of modern life and the impersonal nature of our society, its market places and its government services and other spheres of activity, have taken away responsibility from the individual and removed power from the people. It is not simply that responsibility and power have been taken over by someone else that we can trust or even know, but the dilemma of the modern situation is that no one seems to be responsible, nobody is accountable. Yet in spite of that, a person is sometimes surprised by the vitality of human emotions and the insight of individuals whenever we can get close to one another. I have had that kind of revelation in the preparation of this book and in the corresponding swirl of emotions in Canada as we seek to find our way together. Rene Levesque has continued to be more accessible and open and even supportive than one would normally imagine possible, and I thank him for his little greeting and kind words, supplied as a blurb for the back of our dust jacket. His openness and sincerity on the issue have only been matched by that of Bill Bennett. In these important times it takes a special kind of political courage to be open to a creative future. I am of course especially grateful to the grand old man of British Columbia, W.A.C. Bennett who is as different in political style from his son Bill as it could be possible for any two men to be, and yet there shines from his eyes a love of British Columbia and a commitment to Canada that is wise, worthy in itself and worthy as well of our emulation.

Then one stumbles upon people with whom new relationships develop that are part of a creative dynamic. Dave Hancock of Hancock House Publishers, was one such person for me. He perceived immediately that we were not marketing books but attempting to sell the country on its own best future, its own ideals and its own destiny. His commitment to that task goes far beyond his role as book publisher. The same may be said of Jerry Forbes, the owner and manager of station CHED in Edmonton. In his role with his own station and his partnership in the Moffatt Communications Network, he has provided me with a forum in western Canada for the dissemination of this third option for our country. Lovers of Canada, commited to their regions, these men see the necessity of contributing the western perspective to the debate on Canada. That perspective has been shared by our local members, Don Phillips in the British Columbia legislature and Frank Oberle in the Parliament at Ottawa. Without concern for party positions or personal political gain or loss, they have debated the issues privately and publicly and have adopted a positive stance toward the future.

In Dawson Creek I have a special circle of friends who have contributed to my thinking on this particular issue. My chief collaborator has been my wife Jenny who wakes me up in the middle of the night to argue with me. Lately, so have some of my other friends, via telephone. Chief among them are Martin Hunter, a district farmer, Alan Jakeman, my physician and Hegelian philosopher, John Woronuk, dentist and Canadian nationalist, Bill Girdwood, Credit Union Manager and community activist, Barry Moore, College Principal, Beth Schilds, my Pastoral Associate, and Millie Best who typed bits and pieces whenever Jenny gave up on me. There is Larry Lewin, lawyer and economist as well as Don and Shirley Marshall who have been with the project from the beginning. To all of these people and to many others, for private conversations and valued letters and reactions on open line shows, I express my deepest personal thanks. It's been fun to get this thing together but we have all sensed the urgency and the importance of the task. It is my hope that the readers will not simply enjoy what we believe to be a good book, but that each one will make the task his own from this point forward.

Brian Brown
Dawson Creek
Canada Day 1977

Books by Brian A. Brown

The Sacramental Ministry
The B rning Bush
Separatism
The New Confederation

CONTENTS

W.A.C. Bennett
Premier of British Columbia
1952-1972

FOREWORD

The reason we had for suggesting five regional provinces several years ago was that we realized at that time that certain problems were facing Canada. Canada is half a continent in size, just like the United States except that we are more spread out than they are. We have distinct problems and opportunities and five distinct regions: One—the Atlantic region; Two—the Quebec region; Three—Ontario; Four—the Prairies, and Five—the Pacific region.

The British North America Act gives more powers to the provinces than they are now exercising. We would have brought the powers back to the regions.

The main revenue that any government must use for the raising of the standard of living of ordinary people is the income tax and the corporation tax. Under our constitution such direct taxation belongs to the provinces. In 1917 when we were under a wartime government, and everyone wanted to win the war, Sir Thomas White, then the Minister of Finance in the Conservative Government, brought in the Federal Income

Tax under the War Measures Act. He made it very clear in the House of Commons that this would only be in duration to apply for the war. When the war was over the federal government would be barred from that field because that field was provincial. But after the war they occupied it more and after the second war they occupied it more again until they thought they owned that field. In that sense, it's been a long war.

If we had five strong regional provinces and they had this revenue; then we could give services direct to people without the additional layer of federal bureaucracy. The people would understand what is going on much better. Each region would be equipped to deal with the particular problems facing their own region.

This is the basis of the complaints in Quebec. If revenues were applied directly to the needs of people instead of to the structures of bureaucracy, and if each region was given the resources to handle their own problems, they you couldn't chase people out of Canada.

You cannot have new little provinces created all over the North either, because they could not really take care of their responsibilities—most of our present provinces can't. Trade naturally flows north and south—they should align themselves with us and create strong regions in which they could have a say where it counts.

The five regional provinces would not weaken Canada. The five regional provinces would save Canada. They would make up a real United Canada. People are wrong when they think that strengthening the regions would weaken Canada. No way! No more than when you have the same situation in a home. If you have five children, they eventually create five different homes. That does not weaken the family ties; that strengthens them. As a father, and now a grandfather, I know very well the way to strengthen the family is to give your sons and your daughters more authority, not less.

The federal government, no matter which party has been in power in Ottawa, has always sought to centralize authority. They have centralized everything and this is very, very dangerous in a country like ours. In the United States where the Senate has power, you have two Senators from each state, but in Canada we do it by population. Central Canada has the population and so it dominates Canada. They will always dominate Canada under our system unless we have five nearly equal regional provinces.

Still, you need the central authority with lots of power in a few areas—to deal with the defence of Canada in an emergency, to deal with foreign trade and to deal with currency and the like.

To go beyond that is unnecessary and smothers the initiative of each region. Take every small business; they have to fill out so many federal forms and reports because the federal bureaucracy wants to find out everything about what is going on in every part of the country, even in things that do not concern them, under the consititution. Small business cannot afford that and it breaks down initiative. Every individual, too, must be able to see beyond the end of the tunnel and see some light, some opportunity—and bureaucracy has killed this.

Central Canada gets all the benefits from the present confederation, yet I would never want to see British Columbia leave confederation. The rest of the country would actually collapse now without the west. Central Canada gets all the advantage of tariffs because of their political strength and all the advantage of freight rate structures because of their central position and because they can ship both east and west to people who are bound to trade with them. Moreover, the federal government, the biggest business in the land now, does all of its basic supply purchasing in central Canada—with our money.

The system used in the United States will not work here either. Canada is not the United States, although our closest friend and partner will always be the United States. We have to have a system of government and an economy that is suitable for Canada—that is strong regional governments.

I have lived in the Maritimes and on the Prairies and here in British Columbia. Many easterners cannot grasp the potential of our western regions because too few of them have ever been out here. When I was a young man, back in the Maritimes, I had no idea of the greatness of British Columbia or of the Prairies. I had to come and see it for myself. As a young boy in New Brunswick I remember the men during the harvest period would take the excursion trains to Alberta, Saskatchewan, or Manitoba, to work in the harvest. They would come back with the story of the wonderful prairies, about the black loam and enormous crops. Nobody believed them. Later on when I would go back and tell the folks what was going on in British Columbia they would not believe me either.

But there is no problem in Quebec or the Maritimes that the people there could not solve if they were given the chance. If we had the five strong regions, Quebec would automatically have everything they want now; all the basic rights would be there within that regional province of Quebec. They could still be part of Canada and receive the benefits from belonging to this wider association. Every other region would have the same power and authority. You cannot have a different treatment for one region than another. In the same way you cannot treat one son or one daughter different from another.

Mr. Brown, it may be late but it will never be as early again. The time to act is now. You get this book out and then you go back to the Maritimes and advocate the rights of that region there, to get their act together. Don't ask their opinion but show what great benefits there would be for them if they acted together as a region and got back all their rights. Do the same in Quebec, the same in Ontario, and the same on the Prairies. Tell your story everywhere. This book must not be the end of it. This is the beginning. You have the vision; no way can you turn your back on it.

W.A.C. Bennett
Kelowna, British Columbia
May 24, 1977

PART ONE

NEITHER SEPARATISM
NOR FEDERALISM

1

THE THIRD OPTION

The third option for Canada has begun to take shape at last. The log jam of emotions between those who support the extremes of separatism and those in favor of highly centralized federalism is about to be broken by creative leadership from Western Canada. The concept of Canada as a Union of Sovereign Provinces holds the promise of a new Confederation to replace the old system which has become more of a federation than a confederation. Provincial sovereignty will give Quebec everything it wants, or at least everything it really needs along with better future options for Atlantic Canada, Ontario and both the North and the West. The fathers of this new Confederation might be provincial leaders like Peter Lougheed and the present Premier of B.C., Bill Bennett, who will find the separatist, Rene Levesque, rallying to their standard in order to save his own position and the federalist, Bill Davis, joining in because any kind of Canada is better than no kind of Canada for Ontario.

Two weeks after the Quebec election, Premier Lougheed was interviewed for the Toronto Globe and Mail. At the same time, Premier Bennett was visiting in my home in Dawson Creek where we recognized in Premier Lougheed's remarks the beginnings of a position that has been held by British Columbia for some time. A couple of months later, on the CTV program "Question Period", Premier Bennett began to articulate his own position. Taken together, along with comments both leaders have made to me after they read the first draft of my manuscript for *New Confederation*, a definitive third option for Canada emerges.

Neither British Columbia nor Alberta is unalterably committed to Central Canada, especially under the kind of federal system we have known until now. Premier Levesque will take courage from that except that these Western leaders correctly identify the feelings of their people, and most probably also the feeling of the majority of Quebecers, when they insist that the best of all possible options is the building of a new kind of Canada. This is now an urgent task but there is still time. Premier Lougheed says:

"Alberta would separate only as a last resort to protect its own interest. Such a situation could arise under a future premier less moderate than myself".

Premier Lougheed recognizes the growing sense of alienation and frustration which is resulting, in the growth of separatist groups in Alberta.

"I am usually regarded as a pretty strong advocate of Western views, but increasingly I find myself very much a moderate compared to some of the intense feelings being expressed. The feelings are getting very, very intense. That is what I am trying to avert and what I am saying and what I am trying to communicate to Central Canada. There is no reason why this country shouldn't be capable of dealing with the concerns of Western and Atlantic Canada at the same time.

The matter of Quebec is certainly significant, but on the other hand what sort of country do we have, if we had these problems, which we had for generations, in the terms of colonization of Western Canada by Central Canada and we don't meet that problem? Sure, we have to pay attention to Quebec, but I think Central Canada had better pay attention to the Western situation or we are going to find the alienation, already very deep here, getting deeper and deeper.

The patience of Western Canadians is sorely tried. And if, at this stage, just when the West is on the verge of finally being able to get close to its potential, an election in Quebec becomes an excuse for the Ottawa bureaucracy and the Toronto establishment to say, 'Oh, we can now forget about those Western provinces and their problems because they are minor and let's concentrate on Quebec', that I think would be a very tragic decision.

Our problem is the various efforts by the federal government to erode provincial rights under the constitution. We believe that Canada is strong if its regions are strong, and the only way that the regions could be strong is through strong provincial governments. This applies equally in the Western as well as in the Atlantic regions. Part of the inequity of the whole Canadian system is that in Central Canada we have two large provinces and on either side a scattering of smaller and relatively less populated provinces."

Premier Bennett holds the view that a Confederation of five strong regions: Atlantic, Quebec, Ontario, Western and Pacific is the best system of government for Canada. Premier Bennett says:

"Strong regions or strong provinces will make a strong country. The Confederation of five regions is the only way you can run a country of just over twenty million people with the size of Canada. It is only when you've got weak provinces that you've got dissent and discord and people looking for solutions that I don't think are the answer, and that is 'break the country up'. It would not be breaking up the country to allow those areas to solve their own economic problems or their cultural problems and stay together in a wider union on some of the larger questions."

Premier Bennett is also aware of the rising tide of separatist feeling in British Columbia. He realizes that it is in reaction both to events in Quebec and to the kind of unworkable bureaucratic federalism that is no longer acceptable to the West. He recognizes that in the concept of sovereign provinces representing the five regions of Canada there exists the best of all possible futures for his region. Bennett says:

"If we were to become a separate country by ourselves, we would be a landbridge between Alaska and the continental United States. Existing alone as we would be, their eyes would be on joining the two parts of their country together. Those who think we don't have an opportunity in Canada as a province should look at the very limited opportunities we would have as an independent country or as a state in the United States. Even in the event of Quebec's withdrawal from Confederation, I would still say to British Columbians, 'Stay part of Canada'. But I don't think it has to come to that and neither do we have to return to the kind of stifling federalism that has prevented the various regions of Canada from realizing their full potential.

Returning to the theme of a new Confederation,

Premier Bennett makes the point that all Canadians have a stake in the way in which any part of the country is organized. He points out that before joining Confederation, British Columbia was made up of four colonies just like the four Atlantic Provinces.

"We made our amalgamation into a single governable unit before we entered Confederation and we thus don't have such costly government in British Columbia. I understand there have been some discussions on unity underway in the Maritimes for some years but I have heard very little on it recently. It seems like a logical extension of trying to affect consolation. From British Columbia, I am not trying to force it on them, but many people here think that they should rationalize their governments."

No one is committing himself in advance to any specific new boundaries for the sovereign provinces in the West. Most are open to the prospect of studies in that direction, including the other Western provinces and the North. To continue in a partnership with Quebec and Ontario and to allow Quebec to increase its jurisdiction over cultural and economic matters within its own province, the other provinces of Canada must be sufficiently strong and viable to assume equal responsibilities for their own region. Theoretically, if Prince Edward Island can insist on provincial status for itself so can the Yukon or for that matter so could the Peace River Country, Western Ontario, Vancouver Island or Cape Breton. On that basis of population we could be faced with a Canada of some 200 provinces. These nonviable provinces would then seek their budgets from Ottawa and be entirely subject to a federalist system of government in which the concept of genuine Confederation would have no place. The term con-federation really means a loose union of largely autonomous regions. Canada has unwittingly ceased to be a con-federation and has become a federation, highly centralized and under the control of a federal authority and its bureaucracy. That is so clearly unacceptable to one quarter of the country, Quebec, and so strongly resisted by the Western provinces, that the idea of tiny provinces continuing as they have must be rejected along with both separatism and federalism. Only Confederation can work for Canada and Confederation can only work when the larger regions each come into their own as strong Sovereign Provinces.

This is a position that can be endorsed by separatists who simply want an opportunity for their region to maintain its identity and develop its potential. At the same time this position can be embraced by federalists whose main concern is to preserve the unity of Canada. Both federalists and separatists can modify their positions sufficiently for the new Confederation. Both Premier Lougheed and Premier Bennett have family roots in the Maritimes.

If the Atlantic Provinces are unwilling to get their act together and refuse to be a part of the emerging new Confederation, it is perhaps their prerogative to opt out. Yet I think it can be illustrated that Atlantic Canada has lost the most in our present federated system and that Atlantic Canada has perhaps the most to gain from a new Confederation. The rest of us know that we need an opportunity to carve our own destiny and we can't afford as much government and bureaucracy as Maritimers seem to think they need.

The mistake the Parti Quebecois makes is that somehow they have believed that they are alone in their frustration. A few years ago Rene Levesque asked, "How can we be expected to build a strong Quebec when the hammer is in Quebec City and the nails are in Ottawa?" Quebec was just then coming of age but more recently one region after another has outgrown federalism and centralism. The question is now being asked: "How can we build a strong Alberta with the hammer in Edmonton? Or a strong Nova Scotia with the hammer in Halifax? Or a strong British Columbia with the hammer in Victoria—and the nails always far away in Ottawa?

Truly this is not a racist thing. In the West we have nothing against "French only" in Quebec. Rene Levesque has nothing against "English only" in the West. We will all have to make some sacrifices. Canada will remain bilingual, English in some parts, French elsewhere—not both everywhere. This is a different definition of bilingualism, but just as valid. Cultural interchange will continue, perhaps more happily than before. That is not the basic problem.

The main problem for this diverse Canada is the business of the hammer and the nails. Each region needs both hammer and nails clearly established within its own jurisdiction. These regions can then form a union called Canada, stronger than ever before. For federal political parties to lead us off on any other red herrings, such as reducing the crises to simplistic questions of love and humanity, or language and racism, is the greatest imaginable disservice to Canada.

Mountain Region   Prairie Region

2

THE CANADIAN DISEASE

Prime Minister Mackenzie King once commented that, "Some countries have too much history; ours has too much geography." By too much history, he meant that some countries become trapped and enmeshed to the extent that they are unable to move in new directions for the future. The parallel with the Canadian situation, and its geography, is the profound root of the dilemma that is Canada. How do we deal with such vastness and diversity? Mackenzie King's example may be instructive as we face this dilemma in our time. During his tenure as prime minister, by far the longest of any Canadian prime minister, Canada grew and prospered. There are those who would now maintain that he was a weak leader and that his governance of the country under the advice of his departed mother, speaking through reincarnations in puppy dogs and seances, is something of a comic opera. The fact is that during those years the Canadian regions did many great things together. They fought wars and they established Canada's role in international affairs but to a great extent the provinces and regions went their own way in the internal development of Canada.

The West quietly grew and prospered, establishing its own brands of political philosophy and community life. The North maintained its pristine innocence. Ontario built up its industry. Quebec had its "revenge of the cradles". And Atlantic Canada slumbered on through its decline with only the addition of Newfoundland countering the negative impact of Confederation upon the area. Federalism was benevolent and centralism grew only to the extent that the regions desired new federal programs.

In an involuntary sense, that beginning of federal growth was the start of our troubles. The loose Confederation of former colonies, which were given sweeping powers under the British North America Act, surrendered one prerogative after another to Ottawa as concessions to expediency. The provinces were simply too small to undertake for themselves the total responsibility for their needs in such fields as health, welfare, education, recreation, transportation, and so on. Slowly the federal government has become involved in road building, health care, welfare costs, industrial development, unemployment insurance and an endless list of programs that originally fell under the jurisdiction of the provinces.

In 1917 the provinces gave unanimous consent to the federal government to allow it to enter the field of personal income taxation on a temporary basis. This was a measure to enable Canada to meet its expenses of the war effort and was in no way intended as a permanent feature of our federal structure. Yet because of the expediency of letting the federal government undertake national programs in all the above provincial jurisdictions, it was likewise expedient to allow the gathering of federal taxes through a perpetual continuation of this aberration of the British North America Act.

Mackenzie King recognized the problem and under weak leadership such as his, which ideally suited the Canadian situation, nothing really got out of hand. He knew that Canada was too vast and too diverse to attempt to force federalism, centralism, and conformity. Unfortunately for Canada, the governments since Mackenzie King's time have been less and less mindful of our diversity and more and more concerned to build up the federal empire. Creeping federalism continued through the administrations of L. St. Laurent and J. Diefenbaker and picked up tempo under L.B. Pearson. The stage was set for the disaster of the Pierre Trudeau administration.

There are special philosophical reasons for the extreme of centralization under the Trudeau government, to which we will give consideration. Without listing the extent of federal involvement or describing the style of participation in areas of provincial jurisdiction too numerous to mention, let us simply examine the broad outline as indicated by stark statistics taken from the government record as published in the Hansard record of debates of the parliament at Ottawa.

During the decade of the Trudeau administration, the records indicate clearly that the federal budget has expanded from $11 billion in 1968 to $46 billion in 1977. There is no sense in suggesting that inflation during that period has been more than four hundred per cent. We have not fought a war and there has been no comparable national calamity or vast new program such as the conquering of outer space or the building up of civilization in the North.

The fact of the matter is that all this growth has taken place in those aspects of Canadian life described by the British North America Act as falling under provincial jurisdiction. During the same ten-year period, the civil service of the federal apparatus has grown from just more than 300,000 employees to nearly 500,000. This growth in bureaucracy, while less than double, bears absolutely no relationship to the growth of population in Canada during the same period.

Federalism has gone berserk in a country not suited for federalism or centralization in the first place. The twin reasons for this are in the inability of the provinces to fulfil their own mandates and the eagerness of the federal authorities to build up their empire, responding to a particular philosophy which we shall describe. The failure of the provinces to fulfil their own mandates is occasioned by the fact that eight of the ten provinces and all the territories remain so sparsely populated that they are not yet able to fucntion responsibly in all the jurisdictions given to them by the constitution. The acquiescence to Ottawa for reasons of expediency has continued. The exception of the provinces of Quebec and Ontario is obvious, for they are of a size and population to enable them to fulfil the extensive mandate given to the provinces. Quebec has therefore reacted vigorously against federalism while Ontario, as the prime beneficiary of centralism, has not felt the frustration of this backward development.

The main development in Quebec over the last few decades has been a movement toward greater provincial autonomy, as is appropriate in so diverse a land. But running directly counter to that movement has been the thrust of a small group of intellectuals who made their way from Quebec to Ottawa to champion federalism. They were eagerly received by much of the population of Ontario with its profitable centralism. Less enthusiasm was shown by Atlantic Canada and the West who were still committed to expedient federalism but were experiencing frustrations and alienation.

This group, led by the "three wise men", Jean Marchand, Gerard Pelletier and Pierre Elliott Trudeau, was surrounded by vigorous minds and energetic people of the same philosophical background. They have been strengthened since by the likes of Marc Lalonde, whose schooling, religion, and culture reflect the same philosophical stance.

That stance has been described recently in a major work published in Europe. "Le Mal Francais" (The French Disease) by Alain Peyrefitte describes the roots of centralism in French society. Everything in France is decided in Paris, down to the smallest of details with respect to road construction in outlying provinces and even overseas territories. Everything is highly organized and centralized in departments that are run by the federal authority.

Peyrefitte traces the rise of centralization of the state from the intellectual dogmatism and the authoritarianism of a rigidly hierarchical administration which took root in France after the Council of Trent, during the era of absolute monarchy as conceived by Richelieu and Louis XIV. Far from destroying that absolute central authority, the French Revolution simply took it from the monarchy and gave it to the bureaucracy.

Peyrefitte describes the bureaucracy as a state within a state, a state which trusts nobody but itself and tends to reject any initiative coming in from outside. Citizens and communities put themselves entirely in its hands while at the same time they look upon it more as an adversary than as an extension of themselves.

He writes: "How can this vicious circle France is locked in be broken? The people are simultaneously submissive and undisciplined, which makes for' rigidity and a bureaucracy that discourages initiative, stifles life and manages to make the citizens even more dependent. And this until the day when, exasperated, they swing violently from indifference to insurrection."

Peyrefitte gives numerous examples of stifled initiative and bureaucratic bungling in Europe and we could add many of our own. All this is now about to be broken up by the regionalism that will be possible in the European Economic Community. The point for us to note is that while the population of Quebec as a whole has emerged into new vitality and freedom, and is in step with the actual needs and circumstances of so diverse a country as Canada, the "French power" group in Ottawa has come out of the disciplined intellectual stream of the scholasticism learned in Jesuit schools. Dogmatism and rigidity are characteristics of this school and highly centralized hierarchical administrations are the result.

Canadian historians frequently make the point that the break between Quebec and France was absolute following the conquest. Yet the influence of the Council of Trent (1545-1563), Richelieu's policies, and the Napoleonic "reforms" were deeply entrenched in Quebec during the era of New France. This influence has come down to our age through the discipline of the rigid, authoritarian Jesuit education given young Trudeau and young Lalonde. That philosophical stream has seized power in Canada at what is, for it, the most advantageous time in our history. Creeping centralism had been a fact of Canadian life, in spite of the realization that we do have too much diversity and "too much geography" for such a system.

Temporary measures such as the income tax arrangement and expediency in areas such as health care and welfare gave an unparalleled opportunity to those who were philosophically committed to centralism. The federal bureaucracy, a state within a state, with its inefficiency and smothering influence is a natural result. It is primarily against this trend that modern Quebec continues to rebel.

Rene Levesque rejected that scholastic philosphy part way through his education. The rejection of that style of Church life, schooling and government is the most important development in modern Quebec. The stronger Ottawa has become, the more determined the rebellion.

Atlantic Canada, feeling that it has few options, remains acquiescent. Forgetful of its own glorious past, both in culture and economy, prior to Confederation and unmindful of the resources of the ocean that other nations come to reap, and the mines and forests and farms whose initiative and productivity have been smothered by provincial ineptitude and federal arrangements, the potentially resourceful Atlantic region of Canada would rather fret than fight. Ontario has no complaint because of the benefits of centralization but in the West and in the North, Quebec may find new allies. In these regions authoritarianism has never dominated a basic spirit of freedom, independence and self-reliance. If Canada ever hopes to fulfil any kind of destiny, it is absolutely essential that the regions have opportunities to realize their potential.

The attempt to apply the same kinds of unemployment insurance in Newfoundland and in Alberta, and the providing of identical laws regarding foreign investment for both Ontario and British Columbia, are but two of the examples of the folly of federalism in this land. Federalism is the attempt to give all Canadians an equal chance and an equal standard of living but the result is the holding of all regions to the lowest common denominator. Frustration grows in the Atlantic region and alienation grows in the West, and federalism is to blame. Those whose attachment to Canada is more sentimental than realistic object to any change in the status quo. There is the fear of change and resistance toward the unknown promoting this folly. Canada as a whole can only realize its true strength when all its regions become strong.

The absolute centralism of the Richelieu model is the philosophical complement of liberal economic theory. Centralism that enforces whatever dogma or philosphy held by those in power is a natural ally of the economic theories of big business and mass markets. This economic position is identified in Canada with the Liberal Party through that party's endorsement of the economic principles of John Kenneth Galbraith. On recent experience, it may be questioned if centralized economy gives better service and more efficient production. Not everyone is still convinced that bigness is better, for a whole counter-culture thrust of "small is beautiful" has begun to attract many modern people.

The combination of liberal economic centralism and Richelieu's authoritarian bureaucracy combine to cause a particularly Canadian disease : federalism in a land in which centralization is entirely inappropriate. Yet by going to Washington and speaking about goodwill among men, as if that were the basis of federalism, our prime minister, Mr. Trudeau, has managed to convince many Canadians that any rejection of federalism is somehow a rejection of Canada.

In the collection of essays *Friedman on Galbraith*, another noted economist, Milton Friedman, speaks of the British Disease—government subsidization and bureaucratic management of whatever cannot function on its own. If the objectives are worthy and part of a plan toward a recognized goal, this is fine. When lack of courage, political expediencey and long-term aimlessness are the reasons for government intervention, control and take-over, the whole economy suffers. The central bureaucracy becomes a holding corporation for every non-viable enterprise in the country. Soon the weight of taxes drags the whole economy down so that government "assistance" is required for yet another level of failing business. It is as if a patient with a coronary is told by his physician that he has cancer. Both of these can be handled these days but the dangers are great. Canada has the French Disease and the British Disease. Only the great natural strength of the patient sustains this land in spite of this deadly combination in a new disease of our own.

Fear tactics employed by the Liberals, whether provincial Liberals under Bourassa or federal Liberals under Trudeau, ultimately fail. That use of "patriotism" which is identified with federalism may be "the last refuge of scoundrels" and may also destroy Canada. The ideal option for Canada is a true confederation, not a federation centered in Ottawa.

Even if Quebecois reject separation in a referendum, and even if Trudeau is re-elected on his phoney "save Canada" platform, the great need for regional autonomy remains. The other prime minister who said, "The twentieth century belongs to Canada" spoke before centralized federalism took over. The present crisis must be used positively to enable all Canadians to recover that sense of destiny.

3

THE MEANING OF SOVEREIGNTY

I believe with all my heart that it is possible for
Canadians to remain together with Quebec. I don't
want a kind of Canada that either pressures or barely
persuades a large element to stay. But there is a way to
reshape Canada so that not only will all Quebecers
really want to remain a part of Canada, but also that
Western aspirations may be fulfilled, along with a
secure future for the North and its peoples, a better deal
for Atlantic Canada and continued prosperity in
Ontario. This best of all possible futures for Canada can
best be explained through a careful and accurate
definition of sovereignty, a definition that is
particularly appropriate to the Canadian situation.
Sovereignty is a word which many English Canadians
simply identify with monarchy. There is much more to
sovereignty than that. Since the word will be used in the
Quebec referendums, it is now important for all
Canadians to know what is meant.

The word "sovereignty" comes from the Low Latin
super ("paramount" or "ultimate") and the Old English

reign ("power"). Sovereignty, or ultimate power, is held by whoever has the final say or decision-making authority. In the Roman Church, for example, it would be the pope, or in an old fashioned kingdom it would be the king, who has sovereignty. In a democracy it is the people who would be sovereign.

The word "province" comes from the Latin *pro* (whatever sphere of activity or space that is "before" us) and *vinco* ("conquer" or "dominate"). A province is any sphere of activity that we dominate by our expertise, function or position. For example, a lawyer's "province" is the law, a mechanic's "province" is machinery. The sphere of activity that the people dominate by their sovereignty should be called their province.

Yet if the people are to truly exercise sovereignty, their province must not become so large or so complex that they cannot effectively control the government. On the other hand, their province must not be so small as to render the functions of government ineffective. In any case the people lose their sovereignty to inaccessible government or to insensitive bureaucracy or to international corporations and foreign nations.

The Dominion of Canada is the province, or sphere of activity, for very few of us. Federal politicians and civil servants may or may not have such a sphere. Presidents of some national companies probably do, along with certain other unwieldy apparatus like the CBC and Air Canada. Most of us are members of the British Columbia Construction Association, for example, or the Alberta Bar Association, the Saskatchewan Teachers Union or the Manitoba College of Physicians and Surgeons. Our province is in our Province but the basic problem in Canada is that our Provinces are not sovereign and even if they were, only a few of them would be able to fulfil their responsibilities, given their present size.

Sovereignty must be held by the people. Everyone will agree to that, but the people must hold sovereignty in a form that is accessible to them. In a land as large as Canada, with so many diverse regions, sovereignty must be regionalized. There is nothing to prevent Canadians from uniting in a Union of Sovereign Provinces, and the Parliament of Canada can be one of the agencies of that co-operation. But to place sovereignty in a federal capital in a nation such as this is to place sovereignty beyond the grasp of the people. The people then become pawns in the game played by federal politicians and civil servants. Ideally these "game-players" should function as the servants and employees of the people in a state where the people are truly sovereign.

On the other hand, each of the regions which is to be vested with sovereignty must be large enough and strong enough to be able to exercise sovereign functions. The basic problem with this at present is that the Northern territories, the Western provinces and the Atlantic provinces are all too small to function viably in such a manner. There is an upper limit to the size and complexity of a sovereign unit in a vast land like Canada, and there is a lower limit.

Both Quebec and Ontario fit reasonably into the requirements for a Sovereign Province but the other regions that consist of several so-called provinces and territories must be unified to enable them to function in the new Canada which is now emerging. Each is to be vested with full sovereign rights, including the right to withdraw from Canada. Once this sovereignty is clearly established and we begin to list the reasons we have for remaining together, some provinces co-operating in many spheres and others committed to only those programs that benefit them, each paying exactly for what it gets, then the reasons for remaining together will be strong and apparent.

The difference between a federal system and the sovereignty system can be described in comparison with the difference between the charter banks in Canada and the credit union system. When I was in Quebec I was an officer of a caisse populaire, the French Canadian credit union system. On the CBC National News of Monday, January 3rd, 1977, it was reported that the federal government is pressuring the caisse populaire movement to place ''s assets under a federal government control before the caisse populaires could have access to the kind of computerized electronic chequing services proposed by the chartered banks in the next decade.

In Quebec the caisse populaires are larger than many of the chartered banks and the credit union movement is growing stronger throughout the country as a whole. This issue may be the next battleground in the tug-of-war between centralized federalism and viable regionalism.

Most of us have dealt with chartered banks at one time or another and if it is in connection with a loan or a mortgage we know that the people we talk with are appropriately referred to as a "branch" of the main bank. The manager will take the application but it must be approved elsewhere. It is not the cash flow of the local branch that determines how much money they have at their disposal but rather the needs and the opportunities of the bank head office, vis-a-vis investments and profit-making, national cash flow and international pressure.

Many people are surprised in dealing with a credit union to realize that the structure is exactly upside down as compared to a chartered bank. A friend 'of mine recently applied for a loan to develop a business through the Lakeview Credit Union in Dawson Creek. There were a number of complicating factors and so he asked the manager, "What will your head office say about all this?" The manager replied "Well, I'll ask the Board of Directors about it on Tuesday night." My friend retorted, "I don't care what they say, I want to know whether your head office is going to give approval. B.C. Central is the mother of all your little credit unions, isn't she?" The manager explained to him that B.C. Central employs specialists and advisers in every field of financial expertise and that these are available to the local credit unions but that otherwise they do not subscribe to their services nor are they charged for them.

This ensures that B.C. Central is truly responsive to the needs and the requirements of the locals and there is no fat and no room for empire building. All of the locals send representation to the yearly meetings of B.C. Central and elect a provincial Board of Directors. When financial conditions make it obvious that something must be done together, no force is needed beyond a recognized common need.

Now, with the need for instant electronic chequing services over a wider area, and the pooling of assets on paper at least, to guarantee that process, the central credit union people of each province, together with the caisse populaires, are seeing the clear need of a Canadian Central credit union service. Still, the structure ensures that control will remain as close to the people as possible.

Citizens in a democracy need to maintain their sovereignty in a similar way. Because of the complexity of government it is not possible to bring sovereignty all the way back to the community level. But the principle is, that we bring sovereignty back as far as possible in order to give us the opportunity to co-operate honestly, with a clear idea of what we are doing and with safeguards against galloping centralism and empire building.

A need for this kind of sovereignty is being felt throughout the world. It is a natural response to the impersonal pressures of modern life in a technological age. That same pressure is building in such diverse places as Scotland in the British Isles, Brittany in France, Flanders in Belgium, the Basque region of Spain, the Ukraine in the Soviet Union, South Moluccan Islands in Indonesia, Western Australia and elsewhere. It will not be necessary for the Scots to leave off being British, for the Ukraine to sever all ties with the rest of the USSR or for Western Australia to become totally independent of other regions of Australia. Independence is not possible in this age of interdependence. We will each maintain ties, even increase ties in some spheres, with those to whom we have historic commitments, as well as geographical affinities.

All this runs exactly counter to the theories of growth and bigness that until now has been characteristic of our age. It has been a policy of liberalism and goodwill to amalgamate everything and centralize and seek greater efficiency. But that trend has turned in upon itself now. Efficiency doesn't come with centralization, beyond a certain level. Centralism becomes an impersonal, bureaucratic and an ungovernable empire. No one is responsible for what happens and sovereignty is gone both from the region and the nation and we find ourselves in the grip of forces we do not understand.

The president of the IBM World Trade Corporation has declared that, "For business purposes the boundaries that separate one nation from another are no more real than the equator. They are merely convenient demarcations of ethnic, linguistic, and cultural entities. They do not define business requirements or consumer trends".

It is in reaction to that kind of reality that the peoples of the world are seeking to recover a genuine measure of sovereignty. In Canada, the economic theories of John Kenneth Galbraith that big business is properly balanced by big unions and both can only be adequately controlled by big government have been embraced by the Liberal Party. Whether the opposite emphasis on smallness, uniqueness, regional needs and identities is in fact a "conservative" position, or one which can be adapted to socialist or populist forces, we can leave for later consideration. Perhaps it is any or all of those, but for now this helps to simply sharpen our concept of sovereignty.

Barbara Ward, the British sociologist, was interviewed recently on the television program, Man Alive. She spoke of western society having been "built on waste, planned obsolescence and cheap energy". She pointed out that "in the era of adjustment that lies ahead of us all, people must regain control of their destiny. Sovereignty belongs not to those states large and powerful enough to fortress themselves, but to those recognizing their interdependence, who are competent to govern themselves in matters of education, trade and commerce, health, welfare and law, and at the same time competent to enter into treaties on defense, energy and natural resources. They will regulate international trade and develop a common front foreign policy with those of like interests".

In some parts of the world the size and complexity of the group who can exercise that kind of sovereignty already coincides with established national states, such as Ireland, Denmark, Holland and Italy. Where the old national state is too large or too complex to give that kind of responsible sovereignty to people in a form that is accessible to them, then "separatist movements" have naturally developed, such as the movements in Spain, France, the United Kingdom and Yugoslavia. Just such a movement separated Norway from Sweden many years ago and this kind of human need may be one of the more profound factors behind the partition of Germany, with international political forces simply taking advantage of the situation.

In that kind of world perspective, the situation in Canada becomes more easily understood. It is not simply antagonism over the French language that has prompted Quebecers to wish to have sovereignty more closely related to their own region. The main advantage is not even the economic benefits that would flow to the Atlantic or to the West once we escape from the federalism that has become so over centralized as to become unresponsive and inefficient.

The roots of Western alienation and Atlantic frustration are related most profoundly to the insensitivity of IBM, and the impersonal life of a technological society. We, the people, seem to be powerless and when on top of that we are forced to endure economic policies that are not tailored to our needs, designed to please all Canadians and suiting none of us, combined with the frustration of language and culture, something has got to give.

It is not enough for the federal government to decentralize many of its services. We know that sovereignty still rests with "them", not "us". They put the Department of Veterans Affairs in Prince Edward Island but that fails to suit veterans in the West. Moreover we suspect that they may be secretly planning to move out the Canadian Forces Base at Summerside, while the offices of the Department of Veterans Affairs are just some kind of sop to keep the Islanders happy during the next election.

The point is, while the Islanders may make representation, they really have no say. Their leverage would be far greater if sovereignty were held by the people of the Atlantic Region as a group. For political

44

reasons the federal government moves into programs of health and welfare, (off limits to them under the BNA act but such is life in a federal state).

They have set up medicare on a national basis, increased our taxes to pay for it and forced compliance by every province through cost-sharing in such a way that only the participating provinces could benefit. Then ten years later the federal government decides to "decentralize" this program and opts out of a $1 billion commitment. However, in return, the provinces have the privilege of dividing up a $600 million tax adjustment. The remaining $400 million, of course, must be maintained by Ottawa because even though the national Department of Health and Welfare has lost its biggest program in the country, it can't be expected to reduce its staff by even one person.

If sovereignty were in the hands of the provinces, and such an adjustment were to be made, you can depend on it that offices would close and the Federal Cabinet would be reduced by one minister. That is the way power flows in credit unions, for example. They can't afford to do it any other way. This need for accountability is why we need sovereignty in our regions.

The Basques and Britons and Scots will all remain in a part of the new European community just as much as Norway and Southern Ireland. The Atlantic, the North, the West and Quebec will all remain Canadian in a new confederation or Canadian Union of Sovereign Provinces.

This is what the majority of Quebecers want. French Canadians are found in every part of Canada. They spread out from Quebec to explore the riverways, the prairies and the mountains. They called themselves Canadiens before there were any English in this country and Quebecers are not anxious to lose this heritage. But they are strong enough now to be truly competent in all those areas where sovereignty is important. The sovereignty that enables each citizen to feel that he counts and that he has access to power is what is needed by all Canadians.

Even in the emaciated little provinces, whose tax dollars go down to Ottawa to be laundered through the bureaucracy and come back in grants as "seventy-five-cent dollars" to be applied to provincial programs, the people see the results of provincial activity. Any survey would indicate that many more people know their provincial legislator personally than his federal counterpart.

If these provinces had not only the responsibility for hospitals and schools and roads, but also manpower, unemployment, trade and tariffs, foreign investment and taxation, then we would really have an accessible sovereign enterprise. We could still maintain joint services in a Canadian postal union, Canadian currency, Canadian passports and defense. We could also negotiate with our Canadian partners in areas such as transportation and transfer of education. In fact, whereas the advantages of a federal state should be more apparent in transportation and education, it would be impossible for the new sovereign-association to do worse than the federalism we have known in such areas.

In a recent speech, the Honourable Camille Laurin, cultural affairs minister of Quebec, commented that it is the rigid federalism of the Liberal Party which could ultimately be responsible for an absolute break between Quebec and Canada. But even if Mr. Trudeau is able to hold us all together and by force, or fear, or nip-and-tuck persuasion, the fact remains that we could have a better Canada in the kind of Sovereignty-Association scheme I have described.

The federal government will not fool us by announcing federal programs of decentralization, administered from a new high rise building that houses the Ottawa staff of the Department of Decentralization. Canadians, together with people seeking a meaningful form of government in this complex twentieth century all over the world, are now entering a new era.

There will still be an important role for Parliament at Ottawa, a place of discussion like the proposed Parliament of Europe. The Sovereign Provinces will each have a Governor-General appointed (or, in Quebec, perhaps an elected equivalent) and the provinces will have ultimate responsibility for all programs that can be totally undertaken within their region. Five large regional provinces may even co-ordinate such things as education better than ten little provinces and a federal bureaucracy.

Ottawa will have responsibility for those programs to which the provinces opt in. The Senate may be appointed by provincial governments, replacing inter - provincial conferences. Senators might meet both regionally and all together with genuine responsibility for safeguarding the rights of the Provinces. There should be a Lieutenant-Governor in Ottawa and the affairs of state should continue in proper parliamentary fashion in spite of the reduced role of the central government. This Union of Sovereign Provinces will not suit extreme federalists or extreme separatists but it will hold Canada together. Indeed the energies thus liberated in each region will make for a stronger Canada than we have yet known.

The fact that socialists in Quebec and businessmen in the West are responding to the same psychological and other pressures is an indication of how wide the concensus may be. As Europe strives so strenuously toward this goal and as people in other parts of the world feel these same pressures, it is thrilling that Canada has the opportunity to give leadership in evolving something new.

Canada's role in international affairs and its opportunity to find a new pattern that may be of value to Central America and Africa and other parts of the developing world as well as Europe is unique. The twentieth century may still belong to Canada. The opportunity for the unfolding of the most fulfilling destiny for Canada is now before us.

It was a Canadian philosopher who articulated the necessity for the re-tribalism of modern man, just a few years ago. Meaningful sovereignty can best be understood in that context. It may not be entirely by coincidence that these theories articulated by a Canadian will be tested in Canada.

Marshall McLuhan perceived that the electronic media, such as television, would be instrumental in re-tribalizing mankind. But rather than all of us being part of a global village as he expected, it is technology such as that employed by the electronic media that has shown to us all our need for one another as people. The bombardment of information from the media has opened up an even deeper need, and that is to belong to a human community that can experience sovereignty.

If there is to be a Canada in the future, it is not because somebody in London, England, told us we must come together. If we hang together in Canada, it is not because federalism brings us such efficient government. We will continue together as Canadians only when we recognize that ultimate sovereignty rests in the regions and that what we do together we do by choice. When that opportunity comes there need be no further fear about the break up of Canada.

PART TWO

CANADA AT THE CROSSROADS

4

THE LAND OF THE
FIRST EXPLORERS

Halifax is like a woodcut from an eighteenth century
novel. You get the feeling that you are one of the
characters in one of those black and gray and white
illustrations as you walk around the waterfront on a
foggy day. The smell of salt and fish mingled together in
the mist is not like the smell of industry or agriculture.
Even a tourist can be a part of the melancholy gray
experience while strolling around the citadel fortress
and driving among the splendid old mansions of the pre-
Confederation era that are still kept up well in some
parts of the city. Even modern highrises and skyscrapers
cannot break the spell.

I remember that "life in a woodcut" feeling late one
evening as I walked through the campus of St. Mary's
University on my way to Dalhousie, listening to the
foghorn in the harbor. I walked along the edge of a
stone wall several feet high that must stretch for a
quarter of a mile or more. Everything there seems both
ancient and strong. The centuries have come and gone
and you seem to owe a debt to both the past and to the

future. You do your part, and things keep going.

The Atlantic Ocean is gray. You try to think of it as blue or maybe green or even with white caps on a windy day but most of the time the Atlantic is gray. The Atlantic is all around the Maritimes and Newfoundland and in its gray mists there is magic. Perhaps it is the grayness of the battleships and the stone walls and the Atlantic that makes the people seem all the more smiling and gracious and kindly.

I remember as a teenager, some twenty years ago, attending a meeting of young people from all over the Atlantic region. I was very impressed with the delegation from Newfoundland and I remember a young man by the name of Art Windsor. I spoke with him once or twice and heard him address the gathering several times. His stature was not impressive and he spoke with that Newfoundland-Irish accent. Just that year in school I had learned about the royal family in England changing its name from Hanover to Windsor during the first world war. Why they chose that particular British name I had no idea but I imagined there was some tie of marriage or some relationship with others of that name and I was of the opinion that many of the finest Canadians were perhaps branches of the nobility that somehow had been transported to this country.

Through the study of history and social science my illusions about royalty had pretty well all dissipated long before I left high school but I still believe that poor, thin, rough-spoken Art Windsor was a prince. I believed it then because of the fine quality of his ideals and his graciousness to others. I believe now there is nobility of a special Canadian kind all through the Atlantic region.

The Atlantic people are not aware of their nobility. They go their way about their business and the high speed and the hectic ways of the rest of the country will never entirely catch on down here. Maybe some day they will put a causeway across to Prince Edward Island, but for now people still have to use the ferries. That's the only way my bachelor uncle ever got married.

His duties in the armed forces took him frequently from his base at Summerside, P.E.I., over to the mainland. You put your car on the ferry and then you stretch your legs or go and stand by the rail upon the deck. It doesn't matter how bashful you are, you can coincide only a limited number of times with a nurse travelling alone on her duties before you are forced to speak. Then you recognize each other's cars when you see them elsewhere on the Island. You might even get a speeding ticket while racing to catch that coincidental ferry.

Eventually things begin to happen and later on you get married. Can anyone in the rest of the country imagine that things can still happen that way? They do here in the gray Atlantic where the foghorns blow and the people sparkle with a quiet virtue and true nobility lies not far beneath the surface.

Yet in spite of the richness of the people there is a melancholy air that hangs heavily over Atlantic Canada. It is almost forgotten that this was once the most developed part of Canada, a region with a prosperous economy that suddenly collapsed at the point of Confederation. Trade has been forced to move in an unnatural east-west flow so that the products of Atlantic Canada are shipped thousands of miles inland at great expense rather than simply traded with the New England states.

The most prosperous region and the busiest economy on this continent stops short at the borderline that separates New England from Atlantic Canada. The resources are there in Atlantic Canada: deep water ports, people with education and skill, mines and forests farms and bountiful seas. But the hydro power of Labrador is developed by others and transported away. The Portuguese, the Norwegians and Russians have the modern fisheries that reap the bounty of the ocean. Atlantic Canada has been depressed for so long that the people have come to believe that such is their fate.

Perhaps the greatest tragedy of the way we have organized Canada is the depression and frustration of the Atlantic region which has become accepted as a part of the natural order of things by both residents of the area and other Canadians as well.

It is federalism that has all but killed Atlantic Canada. Trade and tariffs that have been designed to protect the manufacturing industries of central Canada to the detriment of those who would sell newsprint from New Brunswick and fruit from the Annapolis Valley and fish and coal and all manner of products to New England. Then in fits and starts the central authority attempts to remedy the situation with grants and paternalistic programs designed, not to suit the area, but to apply to any needy part of Canada. We get a useless heavy water plant built in Cape Breton to fuel nuclear plants for any part of the world that buys Canada's nuclear reactors while Cape Breton utility bills remain the highest in the country. The resources and the energy and the people of the Maritimes are all out of synchronization in these federal schemes devised in the office of some bureaucrat in Ottawa.

Believing in their plight as they do, the residents of Atlantic Canada are easily persuaded by their local political leaders that at least they get participation in their provincial governments because there are so many of them. This merely adds to the burden of the people. It is not simply that in an area smaller than British

Columbia, and with less population, that there are 182 provincial members of legislative assemblies as compared with fifty-five for the whole of British Columbia. But this issue becomes compounded when 'we consider that there are sixty provincial cabinet ministers in Atlantic Canada as compared with fifteen in British Columbia and that for each cabinet minister there is also a department and a bureaucracy. Atlantic Canada is saddled not only with federalism in all its glory but also four provincial departments of agriculture, four provincial attorneys general, four provincial departments of health, departments of welfare, energy, environment, and the works.

To eradicate the Canadian disease that is federalism that cannot be made to work in so diverse a country, and to organize the people and the resources of Atlantic Canada in a way which can take advantage of natural markets, and to diminish the size of the provincial government apparatus by approximately seventy-five per cent, would be three initial but major steps for Atlantic Canada to get its act together. In spite of these major handicaps, the region has not really done all that badly but the assumption that Atlantic Canada could not do much better is one of the great tragedies of the way Canada functions at present.

5

JE ME SOUVIENS

Quebec is a region that looks to the future, but it is also a province of Old World charm. The motto, "I remember" applies not merely to the French Canadian majority and their recollections of Quebec's beginnings as New France, but also the reminders of old cultures from all over the world. Each of them maintains its own dignity and heritage and each also brings its commitment to Canada and its efforts toward integration without the loss of those things that make each group unique.

Quebec is a place of autumn leaves and scampering squirrels, even in the big cities. I remember standing on the steps of the Musee des Beaux Arts in Montreal on a windy day in the autumn. The many-colored leaves swirled all around the steps and then made piles off to each side. As I stood there and mused I felt I could have been on the steps of a public building in any of the cosmopolitan cities of the world, especially of Europe. Later during brunch at a Brittany pancake house on the Rue de la Montagne I mulled it over some more and wondered to myself if there is any city in the world so truly cosmopolitan.

Somehow the people of various ethnic backgrounds are not as much confined to their ghettos in Montreal as in London, New York or Toronto. There are synagogues for the Portuguese and Spanish-speaking Jews in Montreal and in a second hand shop you can buy a genuine icon of some Orthodox tradition and you know it is real because it combines the ugly and the sacred in most authentic beauty.

It is certainly true that the city of Montreal is eighty-one per cent French-speaking. The French now wish to exercise the influence normally accorded a majority in a democratic system, but the French are well intertwined with the immigrants from all over the world. Many of these people have been in Montreal for generation upon generation. Just as they would not tolerate the arrogance of the Liberal Party, so too they could play a major role in opposing the Parti Quebecois if its policies are not sufficiently flexible and humane in the future. Every party must recognize that the metropolitan society in Quebec is a mixed society and will remain so regardless of the political future of Canada.

From my own limited perspective, I have been amazed at the spectrum of churches of my denomination in Montreal. Most English Canadians would be surprised to know that Montreal is our largest Presbytery with 119 United Churches. There are many English speaking United Churches in most parts of the city and there are French United Churches scattered here and there. There is a United Church formed many years ago by American expatriates and a United Church consisting entirely of Mohawk Indians. There are United Churches whose members are entirely drawn from the black community, a Japanese congregation as well as Chinese and Korean congregations. There are United Churches worshipping every Sunday entirely in Hungarian, Italian, Armenian and Polish. Like the leaves swirling on an autumn day, their many traditions blend in a three-dimensional mosaic. It is the people of Montreal who make this city so special.

Yet here again Canada faces its dilemma. It is the city of Montreal and the province of Quebec that have brought to a head the essential problem of federalism in Canada. The Canadian disease has caused special suffering in Quebec because with its cultural as well as its economic needs for separate opportunities and development, the French Canadian majority of this province has been the first to recognize how inappropriate the federal system is for this country.

I was in Montreal a few days after the election of the Parti Quebecois government on November 15, 1976. Premier Levesque, a friend for many years, had given advice and encouragement during my preparation of the book *Separatism* and he had contributed an article as the foreword. However, we were eager to have his thoughts following the election and to have the whole thing updated and revised in the light of this development. Some of that had been done by phone but the publisher was adamant that the whole revised foreword be signed by Premier Levesque before the book was released. Once that was done I began to take unbound media copies to some of the press people.

My first stop was the Montral Star. I presented the book to the reviewer, John Richmond, in an unbound form which he practically devoured before my very eyes. Then I went on to the ad clerk. Simply acting as an agent on behalf of the publisher, I asked for one display ad five columns wide by three inches deep and was told that would be ninety-seven dollars per insertion. The man behind the desk continued, "May I see a copy of the ad please?...Oops...*Separatism*, eh? This will have to go upstairs to our censor. Up to the sixth floor, please, and ask for Mr. Walker. Show it to him."

Reaching the sixth floor, I found that Mr. Walker was "Out". The girl was expecting me."Are you the man about the *Separatism* ad? Yes? Well, could you come back tomorrow?"

I explained that I was leaving for Ottawa at seven-thirty in the morning and thence to Toronto and points west, and I insisted on seeing someone else. A dear lady, who obviously had a great deal of seniority, appeared next to look at the ad and then to disappear. After a conference somewhere she returned and sat down and explained very sweetly how delicate these matters had become. If I would just leave the ad with her they would be in touch. Sensing that rejection would be as good as "banned in Boston", I pressed on: "Sorry, if you cannot accept the ad, could you simply sign it and mark it rejected?" The dear lady disappeared again.

Invited into the executive offices of Mr. Alec McLaren things took a new twist. Informed that the initial price quoted was from the retail price list, given me in error, I then learned that "the proper price for publishers" was actually $305 per insertion. Well-heeled and undaunted, I again persisted, reducing the ad's size slightly and reaching the price of $225. I then indicated that I would place an order for a series of ads and pay in cash. At this point, Mr. McLaren became even more "helpful". "Leave the ad with me and I will personally take it to some of our creative people to dress it up as a real teaser. Phone me just before five and I will tell you what we have done."

At that point I left the offices of the Montreal Star with a mixture of amusement and exasperation. Reaching the Montreal Gazette, I offered a copy of the unbound edition for their reviewer and purchased an advertisement identical to the one I had offered to the Montreal Star. This time I experienced no difficulties whatsoever. Then at ten minutes before five I phoned Mr. McLaren, who was "busy in a meeting". At five-to-five I phoned again to learn that Mr. McLaren was "out of the office but in the building somewhere". At five o'clock no one was answering the phone in Mr. McLaren's office. I caught a plane to Ottawa early the next mornng but my experiences in Montreal remain indicative of the ambivalence of people toward the issue of Canada's future. There is paranoia in some circles and there is business as usual elsewhere.

Prime Minister Trudeau has said rather clearly that should some kind of separation take place the people of Quebec should not count on the possibility of any future association with the rest of Canada. To the extent that Quebec is simply spearheading the drive toward autonomy, most other regions of Canada may want to have something to say about that. Atlantic Canada needs greater autonomy. The West needs greater autonomy. The North needs greater autonomy. What none of us needs right now is the kind of all-out confrontation that people protecting federalism seem to want. There are many of us in the regions who could more happily picture a future Canada without Ottawa than a future that purposely excludes any relationship with Quebec.

It really is not quite possible for Quebec to achieve all its aspirations within the confines of the present so-called Confederation, administered by Ottawa. But it is entirely within the realm of possibility that Quebec's aspirations, the development of its own cultural life, more honest government and less dependence on equalization grants from other parts of Canada, together with new policies on immigration, manpower and employment, foreign investment, and the recovery of jurisdiction over health, welfare, labour and such fields could be undertaken by Quebec as one partner in a new Confederation in which each of Canada's regions has greater opportunities in these areas.

6

THE GOLDEN TRIANGLE

That part of Ontario that is called the "golden triangle"sticks down on the map as the southernmost part of Canada. Whenever I look at a map of Canada I am reminded of the shape of a funnel, for under the present set-up, at least, the wealth and the resources of the whole country do somehow seem to funnel down into the "golden triangle".

It is natural, then, that anything that threatens the status quo of Canada's organization will be resisted by those who have the most to gain from the way things are. Prime Minister Trudeau's first big rallies in opposition to separatism have taken place in the "golden triangle" of Ontario. There he could depend on huge crowds and chanting partisans all responding to his plea to keep Canada united, by which he means keep Canada in the present federal centralized system.

Albertans and British Columbians bear no ill will toward Quebec at all. That point is greatly misunderstood. Had the Prime Minister attempted to begin his campaign in Edmonton, Calgary, or

Vancouver he would have found a great deal more hesitation. We don't want Quebec out but we strongly resist federal programs of bilingualism and biculturalism along with federal arrangements for freight rates and industry and everything else they control but don't understand.

In Ontario they don't like the way the bilingualism issue is being handled either, but Ontario is so enamoured of federalism that Ottawa may even succeed in forcing its unpopular bilingualism policies as the price for maintaning the status quo. That is not good enough for the rest of the country and the people of Ontario may have to recognize that fact also. Nobody is anxious to take anything away from Ontario but as the younger parts of Canada come of age they insist more and more upon a different kind of arrangement between the Canadian regions.

Actually Ontario is a great place, even taken just by itself. With a population soon to approach 10,000,000 people, Ontario has a viable internal market of its own. Ontario has an area of nearly 500,000 square miles and an economy that is built on an ideally diversified agricultural-industrial base. Manufacturing is the largest industry but the annual value of mineral production is two and one half billion dollars and the cash receipts from farming are also two and one half billion per annum. Ontario Place is the North American Taj Mahal and the Canadian National Exhibition is the largest of its kind on the continent. City Hall in Toronto gives architectural expression to the persistent efforts at making Toronto a clustered community in spite of its size. The Canadian National Tower is the tallest building in the world. The prosperity of this giant of Canadian Confederation should no longer depend on subsidies from Alberta by way of cheap energy. If the markets of Ontario cannot stand on their own by now we should no longer expect the poor Atlantic provinces to be forced forever to buy manufactured goods from Ontario and ship their resources to this remote and unnatural market.

Just as the Atlantic and the West have nothing against Quebec, it is also true that there is nothing really against Ontario. If we are not simply envious of Ontario's strength and prosperity, we are sometimes painfully aware that we make it all possible. Up to this point that feeling has taken little form other than snide jokes, such as the one about the prizes for the Miss Calgary beauty contest. First prize is a one-week paid vacation in Toronto. Second prize is a two-week paid vacation in Toronto.

But the time for joking is finished now and there are some major adjustments that must be made. Ontario may be willing to make some adjustments to Quebec as a way to keep the status quo for the future. If Canada is to survive meaningfully beyond some kind of emotional vote of confidence in the next election, adjustments must also be made which allow the other regions to come into their own.

I remember my first visit to Toronto in which the outstanding first impression was the squirrels in the downtown area around Queen's Park and the University of Toronto. It was wintertime and the snow was on the ground and yet they were not hiding from the elements. Neither were they starving, for the thing which impressed me most was the chubby appearance of the squirrels. They obviously were sharing in the good life of the most prosperous large city in Canada. Are there such quantities of nuts on the ground from the downtown trees? Is the garbage in the back alleys of Toronto so nutritious? Does the government have some feeding program for squirrels in the city of Toronto?

They used to call it Toronto The Good. In spite of

what people in the media say and the crazy things that happen on Yonge Street, it is still Toronto The Good. The streets are clean and the shopkeepers courteous and seemingly honest. True, the immigrant communities seem to swarm together more here but, as we see on television, the good people of Kensington bring their own virtues to the neighborhood of the old "white Anglo-Saxon protestants", many of whom have established new homes in the suburbs. Perhaps the people in Toronto are not any better than the rest of us. It may just be the good life they have that makes it seem so.

Those squirrels seem almost to reflect the realities of the nation. Squirrels in Atlantic Canada are so small and thin. Oh, they are fine, intelligent squirrels but they don't have it so easy. In Quebec the squirrels are healthy and sleek, and they have a glow of quality in their fur. The chubby squirrels of Toronto just make you smile for their good fortune. Out West we don't call the big fellows squirrels. We call them badgers but they are surely related to their cousins.

7

THE LAND OF THE HUDSON'S BAY COMPANY

It is ironic that the eastern part of the Prairies and the eastern Arctic are regarded by many Canadians as a "have-not" region. The area around the Hudson Bay, including Manitoba, Saskatchewan, the district of Keewatin and the islands of the eastern Arctic could only be a "have-not" region if frustrated by a system as inappropriate as Canadian federalism. This is a region that has natural gas on Ellesmere Island and iron ore on Baffin Island. There is uranium in the barrens of Keewatin and at five important locations in Saskatchewan. Saskatchewan has oil and potash, Manitoba nickel and other minerals. Too, they have grains and cattle and virtually every resource including a worthy people that can make this region vibrant and strong, if given an opportunity.

There are symbols everywhere of human involvement as a partner in the natural order of things. Human beings have broken the land to make their daily bread. Human beings have reached far down into the earth to pump out some of its energy. The Prairies have been good to Canada and human settlement has happened for the most part at a time when humankind has learned also to care for the land. The development of the North takes place in that context. Things have not always been easy here and both natives and immigrants need a new measure of control and autonomy if this region is ever to reach its potential.

The story begins with the saga of the roaming bands of Indians, harvesting in their own way, vying with one another for survival. Then there were the trappers and traders, accompanied by the first missionaries who established schools and hospitals. It is easy to criticize their contribution but nearly impossible to match their devotion and concern. Then came the sodbusters, first French and Scots and then from all over the world, breaking the land with wooden ploughs but doing so with an ordered sense of destiny and community building. They were here to stay, and they knew it. Even since the beginning of this century they built up food stocks and energy supplies without which the rest of the country could not exist as it does today. But where else in the world has development been so orderly that almost anywhere between Ontario and the mountains you can figure the exact speed of an airplane just by looking down and counting the quarters and sections of land you pass in sixty seconds? Marked off in square miles and quartered accordingly, the land bespeaks the partnership between man and his environment. Ten sections a minute means that you are travelling at exactly 600 miles an hour.

There have been setbacks, too. The Great Depression was felt more on the Prairies than anywhere else in Canada. I served a congregation once near the border between Saskatchewan and Alberta and even as late as the early 1970's the effects of the Depression were still being felt. Those effects were no longer economic but psychological, for while the people were doing very well they were so careful with everything they had that they were hardly free to live at ease or to enjoy the fruits of their labors. One of my parishioners once said to me that he had come to realize he would die rich but that he was living poor since he could never really bring himself to eat out at a restaurant with his family and he never felt he could afford a vacation. He was always in dread that those years of the Depression might return, and he wanted to be prepared.

As a pastor in such a community you go through a depression of your own, which in many cases really is more economic than psychological. My predecessors in the ministry there and those who came after me have found it necessary for both husband and wife to be gainfully employed. That is not so bad, of course, but our children were young and we made a decision to opt for an old fashioned lifestyle with Jenny at home and our manse serving as a center for part of my ministry.

On our last Christmas there, my wife was unable to scratch a dollar or so from her grocery money to buy a gift for her husband and so she baked me a deep apple pie and early in the morning placed it warm under the Christmas tree. She insisted that I eat it all myself and I did so at one sitting. The experience was so precious that I really understood something of what the old timers meant when they said that in the Depression years times were hard but families were closer. You made things for yourself but the necessity of doing so and the value of the experience is something our children may never remember or experience.

Yet in the world we live in, all Canadians could learn to do without some things and we would be more enriched by doing more for ourselves. In the Canada we hope to build we should strive for a happier and healthier lifestyle. We can produce enough energy for our needs, with some to spare for others. There is enough food to go around though we should be prepared to pay well for that and again produce some for others if we can. The caution of the older prairie people has something in it we may all need to learn again in the future.

In the North too there is a commitment to the building of a new Canada and a better lifestyle. "Southerners" do have a role to play in this part of Canada too. Consider the reminiscence of Jean Dyke, a nurse in the North for the last twenty years.

My uncle, a mining engineer active in the North for the first half of the century, visited our New Brunswick home frequently and told tales of Athabasca trails, tar sands, muskeg country, native peoples and campfires, and first set me thinking of visiting the North to see for myself if all he said was true. I was twenty-four years old when I received my first posting with Indian and Northern health services. In 1957, living and working in the North that first year was an exciting and interesting experience. In a six-weeks training period at Moose Factory, given in addition to my regular nurse's training and public health specialty, I worked in out-patient's, X-Ray, OR and dental office, learning suturing, X-Ray taking and development, dental extractions and obstetrical deliveries to prepare for life in a nursing station.

After the six weeks I was transferred to Frobisher Bay in the Eastern Arctic. No doctor was resident in that community, while the only "hospital" was our station of four patients beds and two cribs. Nursing became a twenty-four-hour-a-day job with morning sick clinics, home visiting the ill, in-patient care day and night, emergencies, school and public health services. We were responsible as well for natives in camps around Frobisher and those near DEW Line sites, often having to travel out by plane or by dog team if an emergency arose.

Our interpreter, Ticivik, taught me much of the ways of the Eskimo although he despaired at my lack of learning ability when the Eskimo language was involved. Following him through the village was an experience fraught with both horror and fascination as he cleared a path through angry huskies who cowared at his kicking foot but whose anger and courage was renewed in time to molest the nurse trailing in his wake. Not infrequently did I find myself being rudely shaken awake at night by Ticivik saying, "Come, Jean, someone sick" and together we'd travel in the darkness, me stumbling behind clutching onto his parka tail, to the waiting patient. He used every opportunity, even these nightly emergencies, to educate me in the ways of his people.

It was with the Eskimo, in retrospect, that I have been happiest. Life was difficult for them, more so by the influx of so many white people and their ways to their homes and communities. Nevertheless, they had important needs that some of us could fill and they had important contributions to make to us all. I loved them and enjoyed them so that not even old Pouta, an Eskimo whose three wives had died and he was looking for a white one fourth time round (I was one of four white women in the community), could change my mind about them, although his advances were less than appreciated.

Bush flying lent a certain excitement to the routine of Northern nursing. Fellow passengers very often were a pack of sleigh dogs travelling with their owners to Northern trap lines. An inherent fear of large animals always made such trips a sobering experience. A sleeping bag, too, was essential gear when boarding a bush plane and came in handy on two occasions when the pilot, due to poor weather conditions, set down on a lake to await some clearing. One shared tales of northern living to pass the time and spent many hours playing cribbage in feeble light and making magnificent unpayable wagers on the outcome of the game.

I was married in September, 1958, and Ted's death in July, 1959, found me seven months pregnant with a baby he had earnestly desired and the next several months proved difficult indeed. God was always closer than I realized and I know now that all the years of Sunday school and choir and church attendance were there to help me when I needed it most. I thank my parents for that. By the time my son was a year old I returned to work in various stations in the North, specializing in giving assistance when epidemics threatened the native population. For various short terms young Ted was cared for by babysitters both native and white and we spent longer periods of time settled in various communities in the North and taking the occasional semester of nursing studies in southern cities.

In 1970 I moved to Dawson Creek in Northern British Columbia. In 1976 my responsibilities increased to the supervision of all government health units in the north-east of British Columbia. My church and community life are important to me. Young Ted finished high school this year and I was remarried. Whether we move elsewhere or stay where we are, I have loved all my years in the North. But I can be at home in any part of Canada for I only love the North as I love Canada as a whole.

8

THE LAND OF THE NORTH WEST COMPANY

Alberta has always been separate from the rest of the prairies. Together with British Columbia, the Yukon and the Western Arctic, Alberta was explored and developed by the North-West Company of fur traders. The Hudson's Bay Company had laid an effective claim to all that area we have just described around the Hudson Bay itself and the North-West Company was a rival which gave effective competition further west until eventually the two companies amalgamated under the name of the old Hudson Bay Company but on terms advantageous to both. The great explorers for the North-West Company were Peter Pond and Alexander Mackenzie. They were the first to explore and map out the whole region, but many developments have taken place since then. Today we think of the Yukon in terms of the gold rush and we think of the Mackenzie Valley and the Arctic Islands in terms of the oil rush.

We think of British Columbia and Alberta in terms of big cities and beautiful mountains, roaring rivers and sandy beaches, yachts and stampedes, and crazy high wages for whoever can find work. But there is considerably more substance to the region than that. The region is interlaced with networks of smaller but substantial and growing communities each with its unique stories and growing culture. In the area around Dawson Creek, where I live on the Alberta-British Columbia border, there is the legacy of homesteaders in modern times: the saga of building the Alaska Highway's 1,500 miles of new road in nine months, and the story of the S deten community of politicians, professional people, school teachers and shopkeepers who learned of their names on Adolf Hitler's death lists and fled as a community from Czechoslovakia to Canada where they tackled the virgin soil here in the North and nearly died in the first winter.

All these stories are part of a rich developing heritage and each of these groups has made its contribution to the fabric of our society in a way that can never be repeated. We would sometimes wish for another war so that we could get some more roads built around this part of the country but that is just like wishing our children could suffer through the Depression in order to build their characters. Somehow the trials and tribulations of our forefathers are different from our own and we have our own kind of nation building to do now.

There are those who are critical of the old days, too. There was the exploitation of the native population and there were early wasteful attempts at developing our natural resources. But even in the old days there were human qualities to many of the developments that ought never to be forgotten.

I know the record of the Hudson's Bay Company is not without blemish, but in the opening up of the Yukon and northern British Columbia, after the amalgamation with the North-West Company, I find some interesting history. In addition to the toughness and the difficulties of the situation there was also a very human tenderness toward people and things in their natural state. This human quality is reflected in a series of letters that I found copied in the Yukon Archives and which are reprinted here with the permission of the Hudson's Bay Company. They indicate that our North-West was won by no shoot-em-up policy.

The first letter to Robert Campbell was sent as he set out to explore and establish trade "wherever it was to the mutual advantage of natives and whites". The second letter appears to be in response to a communication concerning the hardships they encountered and the near insurmountable difficulties faced by both natives and newcomers in this Canada of ours.

Fort Simpson MKR
Feb 14th, 1843

To Robert Campbell,

... every man must be well found in arms & ammunition, & I beg leave to point out to you the necessity of being very watchful & careful among the strange Indians you are about to visit. We know not yet of their nature, or how inclined towards the Whites. A cautious, but steady & determined line of conduct at the same time, will be the most likely for passing through the country in a friendly manner. Keep also a watchful eye on the conduct of your people while among any strangers. Let them in case of need be always prepared to defend themselves & you, but allow of no nonsensical parade of firearms or anything else before the Indians. Such can never do any good, but may be the cause of doing much mischief. Train them to a cautious tho' not timid behaviour, and make all orders you may issue, be instantly obeyed & strongly impress on all their minds the absolute necessity of them doing nothing while among the Indians to give offence, whereby a quarrel may be commenced, the issue of which may be bloodshed and death...

Dear Sir
Your obedt. servt.
John Lee Lewes
Courtesy Hudson's Bay Archives
HBCA B/200/b/16/fo.43d

Red River Settlement
5th June, 1843

My Dear Sir,
... The loss of life and privations during the preceding winter, arising from starvation, are truly lamentable...

With reference to the melancholy fate of John Spence and Murdoch Morrison, the bearers of the packet for Peels River, who appear to have been destroyed & devoured by some wretched women in the neighbourhood of Ft. Good Hope, you require instructions as to what punishment should be inflicted on these women. In reply to that inquiry, we cannot authorise any punishment, as beyond all manner of doubt they were impelled to the dreadful alternatives by the most pressing calls of hunger. The natives of that part of the country are generally of a kindly disposition—, especially towards whites and Cannibalism we believe is unknown among them. Such scenes are, thank God, of rare occurence in any country, but they have been known to take place even in civilized society under circumstances so imperious and distressing as in a certain degree to

justify the measure however revolting to humanity &
of which no legal cognizance could be taken. We
cannot, therefore, authorise or sanction the infliction
of any punishment on those unfortunate people,
whose husbands and people fell victims in like
manner to their intense suffering before they met with
our people.

I remain, dear Sir,
Geo. Simpson

Courtesy Hudson's Bay Archives
HBCA D.4/61/Fos 113d, 114

These early pioneers, together with the native
peoples, faced and overcame a harsh environment and
tremendous social adjustments. The time has come now
for a new era of development both in terms of caring for
the environment and developing the human community. In this region, people are not nearly so lacking in
understanding of Quebec's need for autonomy as many
Easterners suppose.

I was recently sitting in the waiting room of our
dentist while he treated another patient. They were
discussing my recent book *Separatism* and I heard Dr.
Woronuk give his defense of Quebec's rights to cultural
autonomy to the patient who was from a community
just over the border in Alberta. He was saying, "You
know how Alberta feels inclined to go it alone these
days. That kind of economic independence is just one
side of the separatism business." The poor lady had her
mouth open and full of instruments and was totally at
his mercy as he continued, "You know that both your
family and my family came to Alberta from the Ukraine
many years ago. Let me describe to you what Alberta
would be like if you added Ukrainian nationalism to the

economic climate you have got in Alberta today. Just suppose that our forbearers came not to escape the Ukraine but to establish a new Ukraine and imagine that they came 300 or 400 years ago before any English or other immigrants. Suppose that Alberta today had a population of 5,000,000 or 6,000,000 Ukrainians with a couple of cities of 1,000,000 each in which practically everybody spoke Ukrainian. Madam, let me tell you we would have some pretty strong feelings of our own about doing things our way. I am no more racist than the next man but I just believe the majority has the right to do its own thing in whatever region it lives in."

I have found the same type of support among the members of the vigorous congregation of the church I serve in Dawson Creek. I never preach on politics, and no one in the congregation knows of my personal political convictions, but on the only Sunday that I attempted to share with the congregation my concerns for Canada as a Christian, an amusing thing happened.

A young Irishman visiting western Canada found himself in the congregation on that Sunday with his friends. I began to preach a sermon with the title "A Question of Sovereignty" in which I naturally indicated that all sovereignty ultimately belongs to God. However, I began with some references to the Quebec election and to the fears of many Canadians, at which point the Irishman got up and stomped out. He apparently went along to worship at a nearby church of another denomination and rejoined his friends later.

He stated to them that this was the very thing that had gone on in Ireland and that he wanted to have nothing to do with any church that involved itself in national issues. They soon gave him to understand that their hope is to avoid what happened in Ireland and that what he had witnessed is exactly the opposite to the Irish situation. Responsible Church and Christian leaders stayed out of the issues there until it was far too late. The IRA has become the representative for the Catholic minority only because responsible clergy and Christian laymen held their peace. We do not intend the FLQ to have that opportunity in Canada. The self-ordained "Reverend" Ian Paisley has become the spokesman for the protestant majority only because of the leadership vacuum among protestant leaders of maturity and wisdom. It will not do for church leaders to hold their peace, to sit on the fence and to play it safe in Canada for there are also in this country many bigots and extremists who will gather support in racist, anti-French or anti-English ventures.

I have had a variety of opportunities to speak about this third option, a new Confederation of strong Canadian regions. Jack Webster's talk show in Vancouver and Alan Fotheringham's Vancouver Show on television, as well as some national exposure in the media, are one kind of opportunity. Even more valuable has been the opportunity to speak and engage in dialogue with various educational and community groups in various cities. One I remember with a good deal of pleasure was my encounter with the Rotary Club in the community in which I live. It was an instructive dialogue partly because, knowing one another very well, I was very relaxed and so were they.

Before going into much of a presentation of the new alternatives before us, I questioned the assembled businessmen. I asked them, "Is anybody here fed up with the kind of bilingualism we have seen promoted in Canada recently?" The nods and murmurs of response indicated nearly unanimous agreement. "That is Rene Levesque's position also", I told them. "You are no madder about this bilingualism than the members of the Parti Quebecois in Quebec. Your position is identical to theirs. It is Ottawa's federal program that you both oppose! ... Is there anybody here who feels we have too much government in this country?" Near unamimous agreement again. I continued, "We have two levels of government that are so complete and all-embracing in competence that either one of them could govern a country. They both have complete departments in every area of our lives from health and welfare to justice and industry; you name it and they have a department and a bureaucracy. Now if we were going to seriously curtail one of those levels of government in so vast and diverse a land as Canada, if we were to restrict its sphere of activity would you prefer to have most of these government services in this region where they are accessible or in Ottawa where they might run our lives by remote control?"

Of course by this time the members of the Rotary were able to see the direction in which we were moving. But even so, there was the same positive response when I posed the final question: "If you had the choice in a referendum between the kind of federalism which has the same laws for every region of Canada, or on the other hand the opportunity for Western Canadian autonomy in some new kind of Canadian union, which would you choose?" The response was a foregone conclusion. Once some method of preserving Canada can be promised, with co-operation on a small but important number of wider issues, then Western autonomy begins to look extremely attractive.

I went on from there to explain to the Rotarians that *Separatism* was written primarily to show the necessity of breaking out of the old kind of Confederation which had become a centralized federation. I suggested to them that such a referendum could pass in almost every part of Canada and that we would be faced not really with the break-up of Canada as such, but with the task of building a new Confederation. I indicated the openmindedness of Rene Levesque and a number of the members of his cabinet, whom I know to be open to such a proposition.

A question period followed and it was evident that a new day was dawning for these Western Canadian businessmen, who have an affection for Canada but a resentment of the way things are being run. One of the men had come prepared to give me a bad time and he began by speaking about the way in which Quebec had always seemed to rip off the rest of the country. He resented the graft and corruption and felt that the equalization payments were not properly spent. I again replied the Parti Quebecois would share his convictions. He then laughed and apologised to me before indicating that he had wished to share his point of view by reciting a poem that he had made up years ago when the family allowance scheme was first introduced. To Westerners the family allowance program looked like a pay-off from the Liberal Party to its French Canadian supporters with their large families. The pay-off was made with increasing proportions of Western tax contributions, a forerunner of modern equalization payments which are used not to raise living standards in Eastern Canada but to support unnecessary levels of bureaucracy. My friend then gave his poem which reflected much of modern Western feeling as well as reaction to the original "baby bonus".

> I am usually not quite so lewd
> But this time I'm going to be crude
> Each time a Quebecer
> Pulls out his pecker
> It's we in the West who get screwed.

I pretended to be flabbergasted and the assembly joined in great laughter as I struggled to my feet once more. However I have a great many friends in this community and I had been forewarned of the nature of the poem. Pretending to think on my feet, I haltingly responded:

Your words concerning the French,
Are words with their own little stench.
If I go to Quebec
I'll tell Rene Levesque,
You're a racist, a bigot, a wretch.

The atmosphere was so good that the meeting broke up in laughter and I knew the Rotary Club had joined the movement toward a New Confederation.

PART THREE

THE NEW
SOVEREIGN PROVINCES

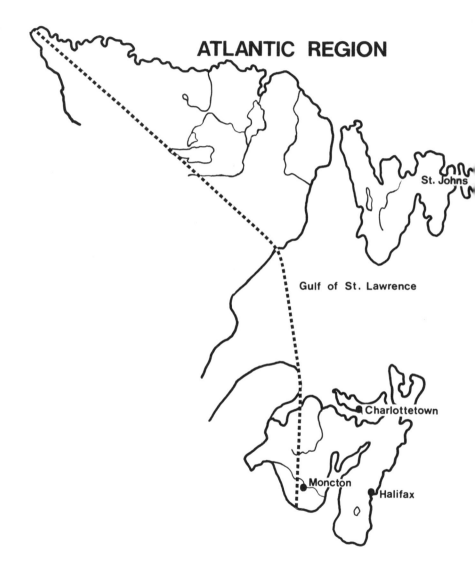

ATLANTIC REGION

St. Johns

Gulf of St. Lawrence

Charlottetown

Moncton

Halifax

9

THE ATLANTIC

Nearly 500 years ago, in 1497, John Cabot sailed into what we call the Cabot Strait and landed on the shores of Cape Breton Island. He raised the banner of King Henry VII of England and claimed this "Newfoundland" on behalf of the monarch. Others had been there before. Unsettled bands of natives had roamed the region; some of them remain to this day, others were on the verge of extinction at the time Europeans began to arrive and failed to survive the cultural clash. Some, such as the Dorset tribe, had flourished in ancient times but were already extinct by the time of Cabot's arrival. In the year 1000, Viking adventurers established brief settlements in Vineland and Markland, now known as the islands of Newfoundland and Cape Breton. Old maps and monastery records indicate that expeditions of Irish monks may also have taken refuge in both Greenland and Newfoundland to escape the terrors of the Vikings. It is almost certainly established that sailors from the English port of Bristol reached the island of Newfoundland in 1481, eleven years before Columbus made his first voyage to the New World. Some of these journeys were not well reported beyond a circle of fishermen and Nordic communities where the rumors originated that influenced Columbus in his view that there was something on the other side of the ocean, perhaps "India".

But it was John Cabot's claim that named the region, established it on the maps and made the reports of the value of the fishing grounds that began the development of Atlantic Canada that has been continuous ever since. The fact that he planted his banner on Cape Breton Island and it was the region, together with its fishing grounds that he claimed, is sometimes forgotten because only the northern half of the region has continued to bear the name "Newfoundland". The fishing was better there and before too many years the English had built up the settlement of St. John's, the oldest city in North America. The southern part of the region was the subject of a longer period of squabbling between English, French and American interests. For a little more than 100 years the southern part of the region was included in "Newfoundland".

Then again for a little more than a century it was known as "Acadia", under French control. For nearly another ten decades the area was known as "Nova Scotia" and then it was divided into three colonies known as "Prince Edward Island", "New Brunswick", and "Nova Scotia". Finally, for the last 100 years the southern part of the region has been part of the new nation, Canada, in which the three tiny colonies have carried on as separate provinces.

All through this time, the northern half of the region has carried on with the name and the traditions of Newfoundland, with its main industry unchanged since the time of Cabot and its capital at St. John's. The chequered history of the southern half of the region has been of benefit in some periods but the history of division has hampered development in the Confederation era. Overshadowed by the huge provinces of Quebec and Ontario, the partnership has been somewhat unequal from the beginning. In the challenging era now unfolding before us this region will have to function as one unit in order to fulfil its larger responsibilities and to become a viable vehicle for the sovereignty of the people. Some time before 1997 (the 500th anniversary of the region originally claimed as Newfoundland) that unity must be proclaimed and made effective.

In the intervening years the history of the Atlantic, in its various parts and under its various names, has been a story of ups and downs. There have been periods of bounty based on resource development and equally good periods influenced by various types of industrialization. Confederation itself has been both a bane and a blessing, for while bringing some stabilization and security by tying this region to a larger whole, Confederation has interrupted the natural flow of goods from north to south. Atlantic Canada has only ever really flourished in tension with New England. In the future, there must be sufficient maneuverability in trade and tariff to allow this region to do business with the American seaboard states. The region has the manpower and the skills, the resources and even the capital to manage its affairs both profitably and responsibly.

It is not true that the election of the Parti Quebecois in 1976 was the first election of a separatist party in Canada. Even after Confederation there was a strong secessionist movement in Nova Scotia, led by Joseph Howe. The movement failed because no viable alternative seemed to present itself, but the feeling of frustration with Confederation has continued to the present time, and with good cause. The continuing colony of Newfoundland also entered Confederation as a Province because there was virtually no alternative.

Even at that, it took a couple of referendums and finally a majority of only fifty-two per cent to bring the northern part of this region into Canada. The only reason that the people of Atlantic Canada are wary of separatism now is fear for the future and the continuing lack of an acceptable alternative. In the concept of a Canadian Union of Sovereign Provinces, the best of all possible futures for this region is described.

The question of the Labrador boundary was legally settled in 1927 by the Judicial Committee of the British Privy Council in London. As we set ourselves to resolve outstanding issues and find a new harmonious future for all of Canada, that question can only be re-opened if it is to the advantage of all parties to do so. I believe that such advantages can be illustrated.

In the first place Quebec makes a claim to much of Labrador (or La Bra d'or as it was originally known) but not all of it. It is generally recognized that the "coast of Labrador" is what was originally claimed by Newfoundland. The coast of Labrador was defined as that part of Labrador facing the Atlantic and those lands which drain into the Atlantic through river systems. It may be admitted by all that at this early time it was not imagined that the Churchill River went so far inland, indeed well in toward the heart of the continent. It may therefore be conceded that Quebec has some basis for a claim, for by no means can the far western section of Labrador be counted as the "coast". However, by legal description of the coast as all areas draining into the Atlantic, Newfoundland was technically correct in its claim and so its position was recognized and given the force of law. Putting all that aside, we will now want to ask: What are the true needs and wishes of the respective regions or provinces? Quebec, which has large investments in western Labrador, wishes to have control over at least the part of Labrador that is economically tied to Quebec. Quebec wishes to develop the area and to use its power as one component in the sovereign viability of that province.

Newfoundland on the other hand has a need for power which is now not obtainable even from the Churchill Falls development in western Labrador. By treaty, that power resource has been ceded to Quebec, which sells the power to New York without regard to the needs of Newfoundland or the other parts of Atlantic Canada. It would seem possible that Newfoundland could be persuaded to give up a few thousand square miles in eastern Labrador in exchange for an equal amount of land on the extreme eastern tip of Quebec, contiguous with southern Labrador and facing Newfoundland Island across the strait. The condition for the exchange would be the provision for as much power as is needed by Newfoundland at affordable rates. The borders of the new Atlantic Canada would virtually then embrace all of Atlantic Canada fronting on the Atlantic Ocean. Perhaps the 64° of longitude could be taken as a convenient boundary all the way from north to south, giving each region or province everything it really wants.

In the same way, if the French Acadians in northern New Brunswick are very interested in being able to maintain their language and culture, provision may be made for the northern portion of New Brunswick to be ceded to Quebec in exchange for Anticosti Island. Both regions are understandably jealous of territorial integrity. Land has much to do with both sovereignty and viability. Adequate provisions can be made for the residents of Quebec who now live on Anticosti Island or in the far eastern tip of the province to be moved to the province of Quebec and to be compensated adequately, just as when industry moves its people from one region to another. Likewise any English families in northern New Brunswick or western Labrador would receive a similar opportunity, and compensation. The numbers of families in each case would not be large.

I foresee a new future for Atlantic Canada as a single Province in which the future will be secure and the people will hold sovereignty in a union with the rest of Canada. Within this Sovereign Province there may continue to be a variety of administrative districts such as Labrador, the Island of Newfoundland, Prince Edward Island, New Brunswick, Nova Scotia, and the Island of Cape Breton. I forsee for this whole region the kind of industrial growth and economic stability that Nova Scotia has acheved in the past decade, moving from the status of a "have-not" province to one of the economic leaders of Canada. There is nothing to prevent the whole region from that future as a Sovereing Province in the new Canada.

It will not be necessary to ensure the future of Halifax and Nova Scotia. They will continue in the economic leadership of the region even when Halifax is no longer the capital, just as Montreal and Vancouver function as the metropolitan and business centers of their regions while the business of government is conducted elsewhere.

Let the other three capitals each take a certain role in the public affairs of the whole Sovereign Province in the future. Place the Supreme Court in Fredericton, the House of Commons in Charlottetown, and the new Atlantic Senate in St. John's. The function of the Supreme Court in the Sovereign Province would be considerably more important than that of the Supreme

Court of any province that we know. The role of the House of Commons would be similar to that of a large provincial government at present. The responsibilities of the regional Senate would embrace inter-provincial Canadian affairs, replacing the Premier's Conferences and ad hoc committee arrangements for inter-provincial relations that we now know. The senators would also have the responsibility to meet as a Canadian Senate in Ottawa, with senators from other Sovereign Provinces, to work out joint foreign policy and international affairs. The Canadian Senate would itself thereby become an important body at last, with genuine responsibility for interprovincial and international affairs.

When I was a boy there was a huge willow tree in the center of a five-way intersection in the middle of Halifax. The tree was a couple of hundred years old and served as a reminder of a distant past, when it was actually used as the city gallows for the hanging of pirates. I remember a radio program called "Tales Told Under The Old Town Clock". The old clock, itself hundreds of years old, still stands beside the citadel and the tales that were told concerned "freelance merchant-men" of the seas who were in many ways the first to claim sovereignty for the people of the region as opposed to outside powers. The tales were mostly true, I think, for they seemed well documented when they appeared later in printed form. Some of them are hideous tales for, once outside the law, people do resort to desperate measures so that when they are caught there appears to be every justice in their execution. Of course, not all these freelancers were regarded as outlaws, at least not by the British. They were valuable allies in times of war. In the War of American

Independence, it was these "privateers" (as they were called then) who ensured that the American rebels never got control of the high seas. I remember the story of how, in a later war, a ship called the Shannon left Halifax Harbor for the old time equivalent of a "dog fight".

The Americans had just refitted their top destroyer, the *Chesapeake*, at Boston. She was now the wonder of the age, fitted with the latest cannon and high masted for lots of speed. The crowds were all gathered on the docks of Boston to see this wonder strut into the harbor when the Shannon hove into view. Through most of the day the "dog fight" continued with the whole city of Boston looking on. The two ships battered each other considerably but as the sun was setting it was the Shannon which towed the limping Chesapeake out of Boston Harbor and back to Halifax with a British ensign placed above the American flag.

Other such battles during the war of 1812 were in fact so lucrative for Maritime privateers that they even began to pay taxes on their booty and on the "reparations" collected from nearby American border towns. It was just such income that was principally responsible for the founding of Dalhousie University, which I once attended.

Since Confederation we haven't even had a war with the Americans to help out the Atlantic region. The time has come for a new vision in Atlantic Canada. After 500 years the time is *now* for sovereignty in this New found land.

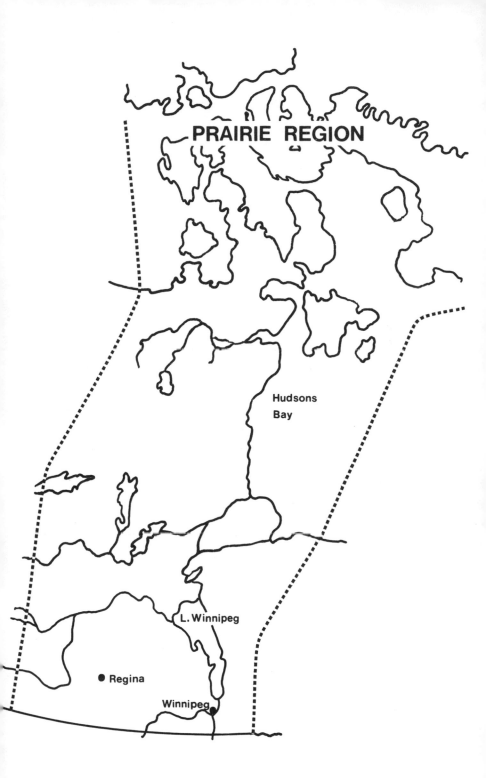

PRAIRIE REGION

Hudsons
Bay

L. Winnipeg

● Regina

Winnipeg ●

10

THE PRAIRIES

About one hundred years after John Cabot claimed all Newfoundland, in 1610 a British sea captain and adventurer named Henry Hudson sailed through what we call the Hudson Strait and entered Hudson Bay. He explored much of the region down as far as James Bay but for the time being no settlement was established and no successful enterprise undertaken.

Even earlier the region had been visited in its northern quarter. Martin Frobisher, one of the greatest English seamen in the reign of Elizabeth I, was knighted for his role in fighting the Spanish Armada. Sir Martin made voyages to Canada's eastern Arctic in 1576, 1577 and 1578, poking into "Frobisher Bay" on Baffin Island and Hudson Strait, looking for a Northwest Passage to India. But the event which unified the region, known for most of its history as Rupertsland, did not actually take place until 1670.

In the meantime, settled society developed in Quebec, or New France as it was known for the first 200 years. Ontario, as we know it, began to take some form on the maps through the efforts of traders and explorers. We may be excused for passing them over in this description of those regions of Canada which have only more recently come of age, for both Quebec and Ontario are well established within their own borders as provinces with an adequate identity. They have the population and the resources to function as sovereign provinces in union with the rest of Canada once the sovereign viability of other provinces is established.

It was actually two Canadian fur traders, Sieur des Groseilliers and Pierre Esprit Radisson, who extended the action into the region around Hudson Bay. They found the government in Quebec too anxious to exercise absolute control over their activities further west and so offered their services to King Charles II of England. In 1668 Grosseilliers helped direct a trading expedition into the Hudson Bay region. The expedition was so successful that the King gave the Hudson's Bay Company a charter in 1670. The Company of Adventurers into Hudson's Bay, as it was known, was made up of English merchants and noblemen along with Groseilliers and Radisson. Their charter gave them sole trading rights in all lands drained by the streams that flow into Hudson Bay.

The center of this empire was Rupertsland, named after Prince Rupert, the first Governor of the Hudson's Bay Company. Rupertsland was practically co-terminus with the boundaries of the recently created provinces of Manitoba and Saskatchewan along with the largest part of the Eastern Arctic.

The region of Rupertsland was virtually the private property of the Hudson's Bay Company for the 200 years between 1670 and 1870, during which the main early settlements were all established. Settlements grew up around the Hudson's Bay Company trading posts and agricultural undertakings in such places as Prince

Albert, and Fort Garry (now incorporated into Winnipeg). The French and Indian cultures developed together into the Metis society and their settlements were augmented by the Scottish settlers brought in by Lord Selkirk.

The name Rupertsland was also employed to describe the region when it came into the Dominion of Canada. The company's control was purchased by the British government, which turned over the region to Canada Rupertsland was governed as one region for a time until it was divided into administrative districts. The name Rupertsland is still employed in some quarters, such as the Anglican Church of Canada, and any other bodies with roots extending back to that era.

Various parties in the region resisted the inclination of Eastern Canada to regard the region as a kind of colony. It was that kind of resistance which had forced Groseilliers and Radisson to sever connections with Quebec and it was the same kind of resistance directed toward Ontario, which forced Louis Riel to attempt the setting up of a sovereign government in the region.

Almost immediately after the region was taken over by Canada the area around the Red River managed to assert a reasonable degree of autonomy in the creation of a small province named Manitoba. The rest of the region was then described as North West Territories and divided into administrative districts, some of which were added to Manitoba in time and others amalgamated to form the province of Saskatchewan. The district of Keewatin, to the north in the Eastern Arctic, remains outside any provincial jurisdiction to this day.

During the first 100 years of Confederation, Manitoba and Saskatchewan enjoyed growth in many aspects of human endeavor and responsibility. They were no longer colonies but full provincial partners in the Confederation era of this developing country. In this era they were unable to exercise any greater degree of sovereignty than they held, and so their development continued under the leadership of the federal authority in Ottawa, which held sovereignty for all regions of Canada.

That era is over in this region of Canada as surely as it is in the Atlantic region. The need for people in this region to hold sovereignty for themselves, even in union with all other Canadians, can first of all be demonstrated by the things that are going on all over the world. People need to hold sovereignty in a form that is accessible to them and viable for them as the main remedy for that sense of powerlessness and as a remedy for the irresponsibility and unaccountability of this impersonal technological age. It is the events in Quebec that have brought this issue to a head in each region of Canada. Far from representing a tragic threat to Canada, this development is the best thing that could ever happen to all of us.

The part of Rupertsland that needs special concern at this point is that part of the region once known as the Keewatin District as well as the islands of the Eastern Arctic. This is the main heartland of the area claimed by the Inuit people as their ancestral homeland. Proposals to make this area, together with some of the Western Arctic, into a new province or territory known as the Nunavut are part and parcel with the effort of the native Inuits to preserve certain aspects of their original culture and to move into the modern world with dignity and security.

In the regionalised sovereignty that seems to present the best future for all Canada, it is obvious that if provinces such as Saskatchewan or Prince Edward Island are unable to function viably alone, then the real future for a district such as Nunavut is within the region to which it belongs. The need to provide government services in areas of health and education as well as industry and manpower and so many other spheres in a responsible and dependable way is as important to the Inuit as to any other group in Canadian society. Moreover, their wish to have sovereignty that is accessible must be balanced with the necessity to make that sovereignty viable. Their influence within a sovereign province will, of course, be immeasurably greater than their influence within the kind of Canada we have at present, in which sovereignty is vested only in Ottawa.

Economists can illustrate conclusively that the lines of economic and other activity in North America flow naturally from north to south rather than from east to west. It is interesting that this truth is further supported by the developing split between the Committee For Original Peoples Entitlement (COPE) representing Eskimos of the Western Arctic and the Inuit Tapirisat of Canada which is the national Eskimo organization that has its power base in the Eastern Arctic. COPE represents 2,500 Eskimos in seven communities in the Beaufort Sea area.

Many of these people have come to grips already with the impact of oil and gas development. They have established local committees of people to improve industry—community communications. They have their land claims proposals ready for presentation. This part of the Arctic is developing more rapidly on its own and has demonstrated capabilities in dealing with both industry and government. There are some within the national Eskimo organization who are very deeply distressed over the growing split, but they are aware of the fact that the situation in the Eastern Arctic is at a very different stage of development. The Eastern claims are perhaps more all-embracing and reflect different long range objectives.

The point that other Canadians would like to make, perhaps, is that we do wish to make a better response to native needs and claims, not only in the North but throughout Canada. These claims can be more readily pressed within sovereign provinces. We would have some regret at seeing the country carved up into racial areas that are unable to hold their own sovereignty.

As Quebec moves into an era into which it claims sovereignty for itself, it must find ways to continue as a mixed society, albeit with a French majority. In areas of the North where the natives are a majority they may expect a dominant influence. Moreover, as part and parcel of their original approval of participation in a sovereign province, settlement of ancestral claims may be successfully concluded. At this time when all Canada is going through a period of change, the native peoples are presented with the best opportunity in modern history for the advancement of their cause. It is to be hoped that they will seize the opportunity to enter into full partnership with Canadians of other races in the regions in which they live. The alternative is to retreat, perhaps forever, into racial solutions which hold no long range promise of freedom and opportunity for succeeding generations of their people.

The quest for sovereignty in Quebec has presented the native peoples, especially in the North, with leverage which they may properly exploit in their negotiations with their neighbors in the adjoining southern provinces. It would be a tragedy if short term benefits won from industries and the federal government divert the native people from this opportunity to join with the rest of us in grasping sovereignty in the only form that it is truly viable in the modern world.

As Halifax has developed into the only real metropolitan center of Atlantic Canada, so Winnipeg plays this role on the prairies. It will continue to grow as the center of finance and industry and its influence need no longer depend on status as a provincial capital. Moreover, like Nova Scotia, Manitoba is not overshadowed by any larger partner among the former provinces or territories making up the prairie region.

Manitoba and Winnipeg have no need of special consideration or favors in the structure of the region. It is the North and Saskatchewan that need to be assured of their relative strength in the new situation. I would propose that the House of Commons continue to function at Regina and the regional Senate for the region be established at Frobisher, the administrative center of the Eastern Arctic on Baffin Island. Perhaps the supreme court of the region may be located in Manitoba, making use of the legislative building in Winnipeg.

This region has been regarded as a "have-not" part of Canada for too long. The territory has the wealth of increasingly important uranium deposits in various parts of Saskatchewan, as well as nickel and other minerals in Manitoba, iron ore on Baffin Island and natural gas on Ellesmere Island. There is oil in Saskatchewan, more than enough for the needs of the region, along with potash and beef and grain, a virtual cornucopia of everything mankind requires.

This could only be a "have-not region in an impossible federal system such as the one employed in Canada. Ultimate responsibility for these resources, and control of them, now rests thousands of miles from the region. Both natives and immigrants are colorful, resourceful human beings who lack only one thing—the courage to believe in themselves and to take sovereignty into their own hands together. To do less is to possess one of the world's first rate regions and develop it as a group of second rate provinces of federal Canada.

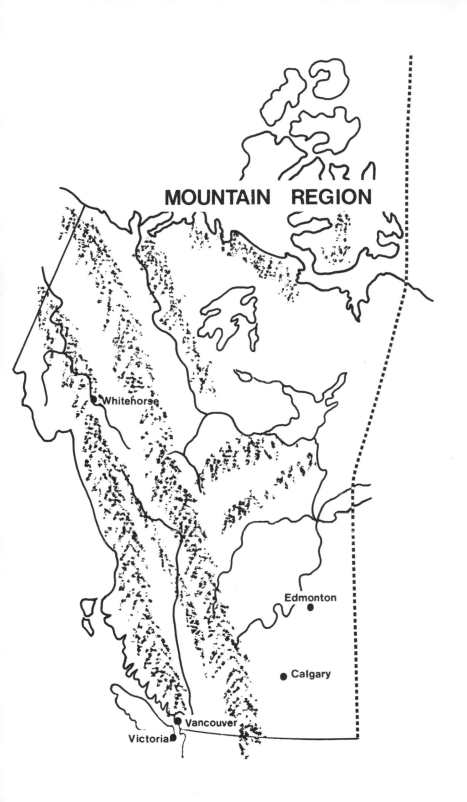

MOUNTAIN REGION

Whitehorse

Edmonton

Calgary

Vancouver

Victoria

11

THE MOUNTAINS

It was yet another 100 years before the third of our proposed new sovereign provinces was identified and unified as a region. Trappers and traders had established a post as far west as Fort Chipewyan, just over the border into what we now call Alberta. The post was under the direction of the adventurer Peter Pond. Both he and his successor, Alexander Mackenzie, were members of the North West Company, the main rival to the old Hudson's Bay Company. Alexander Mackenzie reached the post at Fort Chipewyan in 1787. In addition to his other responsibilities, he made two journeys from that post which took him north through the territories to the Arctic Ocean and west through Alberta and British Columbia to the Pacific Ocean. In both cases he was exploring unknown territory, frequently in the company of natives who knew as little as he did about some of the areas they would visit. Moving down the river that now bears his name, Mackenzie reached the Arctic first in 1789. He called it the River of Disappointment because he had hoped it would take him to the Pacific, but he did succeed in expanding our understanding of the country, the conditions, and the people of the north.

On October 10, 1792, he set off with his men from Fort Chipewyan, again heading westward. The largest part of his journey was made up the Peace River, the only waterway to pierce the Rocky Mountains. Down the Parsnip River and the treacherous Fraser to a tributary which led directly west toward Bella Coola and the Pacific. As they neared the Pacific they began to meet other natives who had traded with the Spanish and who had met with Captains James Cook and George Vancouver and others of the West coast explorers. There were both attempts at trading with these natives and experiences of hostility which caused Mackenzie's men to panic and nearly mutiny except that having reached their destination there was no alternative course of action but to verify their location and return to Fort Chipewyan in any event.

Mackenzie wrote "I now mixed up some vermilion in melted grease, and inscribed, in large characters, on the south east face of the rock on which we had slept last night this brief memorial—'Alexander Mackenzie, from Canada, by land, the twenty second of July, one thousand seven hundred and ninety three'."

1793 marks the beginning of this youngest part of Canada as an identifiable region. It was Mackenzie's efforts that linked the eastern and western sides of the Mountains, the south and north, the Arctic and the Pacific. Some of the developments since that time have reflected the nearly insurmountable divisions within the region, but the region is one in the energy and philosophy of the people, the rigors and challenges to life, and the spectacular environment which holds perhaps the most bountiful supply of natural resources in the world.

There are few Canadians who have even begun to glimpse the potential of the region that has emerged from Mackenzie's trails. Vancouver has not yet come to its peak of growth and activity but has begun to ripen and mature as a city culture. The interior of British Columbia continues to develop and with all the booms that have taken place in the West it is hard to imagine that Northern British Columbia holds by far the greatest potential of all. There is the potential for huge preserves of wildlife in a natural environment as well as resources needed by the human community that are being developed by both local people and incoming industry under increasingly careful provincial government supervision.

Much of Northern British Columbia relates more easily to Edmonton than to Vancouver or Victoria, because of the Alaska Highway that runs north along the eastern side of the Rockies. Edmonton stands to become the inland center of an empire of human endeavor, natural resources and resilient environment practically unequaled in the world. Edmonton is already the fourth largest city in Canada but displays few of the self-defeating traits of many large cities that turn in upon themselves and suffocate their people. With Calgary to the south as a financial counterweight and linkage to the United States, with its natural links to Northern British Columbia, the Yukon and the Mackenzie Valley as well as the prairies to the east, Edmonton's future is to be the center of a vast and dynamic new nerve center of world culture and civilization.

It is interesting to watch through history how the center of human dynamism has moved from ancient times in the first civilizations of China and India, through the high cultures of the Mediterranean such as

Egypt, which fell to be replaced by Greece, which gave way to Rome. European empires succeeded one another in supremacy, ending with the world influence of the British before the center of power and influence moved to North America. For a time it was the New England States, especially New York that seemed to be the center of the world. Creativity, the wealth it engenders, and the accompanying political and military leadership has been passing to the west coast of the United States in recent years, for better or for worse.

That shift is perhaps only a transitional phase, however. Californian civilization and the wealth of Texas and Arizona have seemed to be shallow and phony, a world of celluloid and plastics, of images and little real substance. The real potential for human endeavor is now shifting to the Canadian West, of all places.

If people back East still cannot understand how the twentieth century may yet belong to Canada, it's because they have not begun to appreciate what is happening in this part of the West. Mackenzie's old region is a unit again now. Just as Manitoba and Saskatchewan have shared a socialist ethic of development over the last generation or so, Alberta and British Columbia have developed their own brand of social-conservative political ethics.

The energy and enthusiasm of Metis businessmen in the Mackenzie Valley to the north, the determined spirit of the Yukon and the logic of the Inuit of COPE further north tie the Western Arctic to this region. All through the area first tramped out by Mackenzie and unified by his explorations, the Rocky Mountains run like the spine of a pre-historic brontosaurus of a size never seen before in the universe. The native cultures, the German settlements and the Scots immigrants of old, combined with traces of French Canada and English gentility, are all interlaced with the earthy riches and strength of the Ukrainian culture.

These people have a depth of perception and a commitment to their land that California may never know. The region has a land mass greater than all Mexico. When the drilling is all finished in the North the energy reserves may "prove up" to be equal to those of the Middle East.

This fantastic potential has not diverted the people from some very ess ntial concerns about planned and orderly development...concerns which are shared by producers and consumers, environmentalists and industrialists, to an extent not equalled anywhere else in the world. With a highly productive farming region in the south-east third of Alberta, and the successful commercial fishing industry off the coast of British Columbia, the region feeds itself well and is a net exporter of food to Canada and the rest of the world. The conservationist ethic of farmers and fishermen combines with the economic necessity of such an ethic in the forest industries of the mountain areas and the truly religious commitment to the land on the part of the native peoples to ensure that good stewardship of the earth's bounty is practised.

This region has the perfect opportunity to put into practise all that we have learned in the twentieth century about the necessity of preserving the environment, of developing cities primarily as places for people to live and of using economic and political power to increase the quality of life for ourselves and others in the world community.

The population of this region is growing at the rate of nearly 1,000 people a week and in less time than it takes to organise a referendum, the population here will have surpassed that of Quebec. The government of Alberta is doing everything in its power to use depleting resources in a way that ensures future stability and prosperity as new endeavors begin to take shape. This is to ensure that the anticipation of the people and the potential of the region may not lead to an empty future of broken promise, exploitation and ultimate disappointment. All the components for the best possible future the world can imagine are here, all except one.

In spite of their commitment to the land and despite all that the twentieth century has taught us about human communities and the natural environment, those of us who live in Mackenzie's region suffer from the same sense of powerlessness that undermines the whole community of modern man. We are not sure that our political leaders in Ottawa are actually in control. We don't know if the international conglomerates who would develop our resources can be trusted. The media people who come to visit us from Toronto in their mukluks and parkas seem as easily deceived as anybody else. Our efforts at controlling the future and making it right are undermined by the nagging realization that we do not control our own destiny. Our priorities and our concerns may actually count for absolutely nothing and we do not even know who is pulling the strings or who is in control.

In spite of the best efforts of our provincial leaders, we suspect that nobody is in control and we agonise for our land, our region, its potential and its people. We sympathise with others who face the same dilemma in other parts of Canada and other parts of the world. If they could somehow seize sovereignty for themselves, we would applaud them and certainly, as far as other Canadians are concerned, we would enter into a Canadian union of sovereign partners if we ourselves were sovereign.

The new province of the mountain region must come into being, not as another part of a new Canada made up of sovereign partners. But even our Canadian partners have difficulty in understanding our particular frustrations. Such a simple issue as freight rate structures cannot be grasped by those who do not live in the situation. That issue is simply a visible symbol of the wider reality.

Freight structures are like the tip of the iceberg of Western alienation. Every Westerner who has ever attempted to explain it to an Easterner fails and finds it hard to understand why. We go on trying to say that the Western farmer sends wheat down to the East at his own expense and the Western consumer brings out cornflakes from the East, again at the expense of the Westerner. It is not simply that there are crazy rates that no one can understand, like that it costs more to ship a rail car of corn flakes to Calgary from Toronto than it costs to bring a rail car of steel to Vancouver from Toronto.

That kind of mystery we can live with, but the business of Westerners paying the freight in both directions is simply wrong. The mill in Ontario that makes the cornflakes should pay the shipping costs of the wheat, not the farmer. True, some of those costs would be passed on to the Western consumers when they buy their cornflakes but at least the farm economy would not be ripped off since Eastern consumers would pay their share of the freight from the West.

But unless it's your own problem I guess you cannot understand it, and so we will go on shipping wheat at our expense and consider ourselves lucky to have the sale. And we will buy automobiles, again freighting them at our expense, and consider ourselves lucky that Ontario wants to sell us so many cars. Some of those things may never change but in the future, development of our resources in a sovereign province will take place on our terms.

Canadian markets and North American markets are important to this region but a local market of some importance is now developing. Alberta and British Columbia as well as the Yukon and the territories have already discovered the importance of the Pacific markets. We may have friendly relations with the Americans and a partnership with other Canadians. Our cultural roots may be partly in Europe but it is Asia that needs our goods most and it is Asia that is finding ways to do business with us.

The provincial capital will be Edmonton, with jurisdiction over internal provincial matters. The center for the Senate will be in Victoria, with concerns for international trade with the Pacific and United States, interprovincial and Canadian affairs. The North too needs the presence of functional aspects of our sovereignty and so the Supreme Court of the region can be located in the city of Whitehorse in the Yukon. Because of the vastness of the region and the importance of discussion, research and inquiry, the residence of the Governor-General should be established at Yellowknife as the focus of concern for human and resources developments in the North.

The Governor-General should act as a Northern ombudsman, continuing the work of the Berger Inquiry. The appointment of a native leader, the Hon. Ralph Steinhauer, as Lieutenant-Governor of Alberta has set a happy precedent. The abundance of capable people should make it possible to alternate appointments between native and white Governors-General of the new Sovereign Province.

The acquisition of sovereignty is the final and most necessary step in preparing this region for its exciting and crucial role as the most dynamic center of world civilization in the next century. To close our eyes to this potential, or to pooh-pooh such a destiny for the wilderness that Mackenzie knew, is to line the pockets of thankless, nameless, faceless powers, to sin against the Creator and to condemn a most vibrant people to a future of needless frustration.

PART FOUR

WHERE DO WE START?

12

THE POLITICAL RESPONSE

The bright possibilities for Canada's future are so attractive that one would imagine that any number of politicians would be eager to distinguish themselves by giving creative leadership. Parties look around for issues and they all pretend to be listening to the people. It is only a profound cynicism that makes us all aware that political leadership in this area will be a long time in coming and when it does come it will be in response to other forces and factors. The politicians hang together in such a way that they all preserve their own futures. None of them wants to leave the pack although in times such as these, if any politician or party could find the courage to get out in front of the pack, the people would rally to them and they could actually be the saviours of Canada.

Most clergymen are somewhat careful in indicating their political preferences, because in their congregations there will be sincere people of all political persuasions. Moreover, no political party is perfect and churchmen are committed in another sense to the perfection of the kingdom of God. That is not achieved in any of our lives and will come only as a result of the kind of unique action we have known in the creation event and the Christ event.

Yet while waiting for the kingdom most of us are secretly enthralled by politics. This is because politics attempt to deal with people's hopes and dreams and the fulfilment of human destiny within a limited context. It is therefore, with some trepidation, that I admit to an earnest longing for a conservative alternative to federalism. There is no federal political party now committed to things like smallness, uniqueness, quality rather than quantity, or even to sovereignty of a kind that is accessible to the people.

Somehow the federal Progressive Conservatives have would up on the same side of the fence as the Liberals in terms of economic thinking and centralism. Lately they have been playing politics with us by saying that they are in favor of less centralization, but that is only a matter of degree. There is an essential difference between a federalism, no matter how "decentralized", in which sovereignty is clearly in the hands of the federal government, and on the other hand the kind of Canadian union of sovereign provinces that would reflect a true conservative position.

Many Canadians in every part of the country, including Quebec, stand ready to support the Progressive Conservatives if only they would give us a reason. But to give us a slight variation of the liberal theme is not enough. All throughout this century the Conservative Party has failed Canada. This is why we use them as only a breathing space between successive long-term Liberal administrations. This was acceptable in the time while Canada was growing up and needing a strong federal government. Those years, the adolescence of our country, were years in which the Liberals were ideally suited to govern us. The fact is that we are now in a watershed era but the Conservatives have failed us before and by remaining on their present course they are likely to fail us again.

Professional political analysts might be surprised at this, but a survey would give clear evidence of a startling fact regarding the New Democratic Party. The fact is that nearly half the voters in Canada have voted for the New Democratic Party, or the CCF at least once in their lifetime. The idealism of the party and the obvious commitment of its leaders has been something of an inspiration. It beats down the "waffle element" from time to time and has proved sufficiently responsible to prevent extremists from gaining control of the party. Many of us have given them encouragement, contributions, and even our votes because often enough there has been no one else to vote for. Most of us have even had an ill defined sense that the NDP has stood for some kind of grass roots or community involvement and control that roughly approximates the kind of sovereignty that we now realize we need in the day and age in which we live.

Even the affiliation between the New Democratic Party and the Canadian Labor Congress can seem like a commitment to the ordinary person when that affiliation is manifested in the person of a local member of Parliament who really seems to care.

When I was in my late teens I worked for a trucking company in Halifax. At that time the company was not unionised and many Canadians know that you just cannot trust the goodwill of management in a situation like that. Month after month I was kept on as a "casual worker". Every day I would arrive at the trucking depot well before opening time to be near the head of the line of "casual workers". I worked hard and impressed the bosses so that everyday I was guaranteed a job; they were eager to have me. I was paid ninety cents an hour for loading heavy freight.

On one occasion I was lent to another company because of certain skills I had developed in loading specific types of cargo. I learned from peeking at the books of the other company that they were being billed at the rate of six dollars an hour for my day's work but they didn't have a permanent position for me either. Day after day I worked without so much as a lunch break. I took from home a quart of milk and some sandwiches which, like the other workers, I ate in the cab of the truck whenever there was a lull around noon. Then the company was unionised. I was hardly aware of what some of the older workers were doing, though I too had been receiving advice from management about the horrors of unionism. Apparently, they were going to take a big slice of our money and do little for us. They were supposedly crooked; Jimmy Hoffa was the head of the teamsters at that time and everybody knew he had his hand in the till.

Nevertheless, certification came and among other things the amount of casual work was limited. Suddenly I found myself with a permanent job and the offer of three dollars and eleven cents per hour. Perhaps the odd cents were for the teamster union and hour after hour the whole gang of us no doubt enriched their coffers. But as we talked together in our new brightly lit lunch room and as we realized that the company was not going broke in spite of these new wages, we knew we had been filling somebody's coffers all along. We didn't even mind that Jimmy Hoffa was driving a Cadillac and spending his winters in Forida, because so was our boss.

If that's what unionism means, and if the New Democrats stand for that kind of equality, then we are all for them. The trouble is that over the years, having done so much for the workers and seeking to maintain their position of power with them, the unions have got out of hand.

It is not entirely their own fault, for management has not been open to anything other than an adversary role either. In other circumstances, it might have been possible for the unions to develop from their earlier successes to a new role of co-management of the type that has evolved in Europe. In that case the unions, too, would be concerned about the company's viability and the health of the economy as a whole. As it is, the union leaders have simply sought to protect and enlarge their empires and the New Democratic Party has been sucked into liberal economic theory. In the three-way tug of big business, big unions, and big government, the New Democratic Party has become the representative of big unions. Since it is the bigness of these empires that is a cause of the essential problems of our time such as the impersonal power of bureaucracies and the irresponsibility of technology, once again I find myself without anybody to vote for.

If the New Democratic Party wants to swear off federalism and rally support in the various regions or sovereign provinces, the party may get a hearing. If they want to give us a social democratic platform like the Parti Quebecois in Quebec, and if they want to stand for good honest government, not a stereotyped socialism but more responsive to our needs, and leading both workers and management to a new vision of co-responsibility, there may be some future for the party. To do so they must put sovereignty where it belongs; to fail to do so is for the New Democratic Party to claim for itself an honorable place in the history of Canada but complete oblivion in the very near future.

Once upon a time there used to be a Social Credit Party in Canada. The Social Credit that began in

England under "Major" Douglas, even began with a political philosophy resembling Fascism in the years before World War II. But that is where such sentiments ended in this country and those that bear the name Social Credit today are as zealous as the most ardent humanitarians in the promotion of civil liberties and human dignity for all.

In fact, even the "funny money" theory of Social Credit has undergone a revolutionary transformation. Developed out of desperation in the Depression, under the political leadership of Real Caouette, "funny money" became transformed into a platform of guaranteed annual income—virtually a Socialist measure. Labels are so deceptive, for the Social Credit members from Quebec have no more commitment to the distasteful origins of Social Credit than any other political party. Way back then the CCF-NDP had pretty strong Communist leanings. Back in those days, unknown to us all, the Liberal Party was marching to orders given from beyond the grave, voiced by reincarnations of the Prime Minister's puppy dog. We have no idea what the Conservative Party of that era believed, for it was in hiding then as it has remained until this day.

The interesting thing about Social Credit is that having come through a period of political wilderness, with too few federal members to actually qualify as a party and at one point holding power in none of the provinces, it has begun to re-emerge as simply a party reflecting the aspirations of people. If the labels were taken off some of its programs, such as pharmacare in British Columbia and guaranteed annual income in Ottawa, we would be hard-pressed to identify the party responsible for such a platform.

Take the commitment to a regionalised Canada of five new provinces that is being promoted by some of

116

the federal Social Credit members from Quebec and add the leaning toward Western autonomy of the Social Credit parties in Alberta and British Columbia; mix in a "middle-of-the-road" platform with planks taken from the right and the left, and Social Credit could almost emerge as a vehicle for the sovereignty movement in Canada. If they were to become the New Confederation Party, maintain their populism, and retain their commitment to small business and family farms, many more people would vote for them.

Having said all this, it is still perhaps the Liberal Party of Canada that bears watching. My wife Jenny is a Liberal. She doesn't mind that I am a would-be-Conservative so long as I throw away my vote on one of the splinter parties in the absence of any true Conservative alternative. That way we can go together to the polling booths without my vote cancelling hers. She thinks it is the Liberals who have defended Canadianism in magazine publication, foreign investment and Canadian content regulations in our media networks. Having come to Canada less than twenty years ago she is not aware that the Liberal Party has traditionally been the party of continentalism and that it was the Conservatives, when there was such a party, who sought to develop Canada on its own.

It is fine now for the Liberals to hoist their sails to catch the wind of Canadian nationalism, but without their earlier policies we would not have these problems. Of course, with only minor breathing spaces in between, the Liberals have been in power as long as any living Canadian can remember. The amazing thing is that it remains entirely within the realm of possibility that the Liberals will be able to shift gears once again and remain in control of Canada's destiny. After all, they have become the party of wage and price controls after denouncing them in the last election.

My wife says that is simply because they alone are responsive to the changing needs of Canadian society. It is possible that the Liberals could outflank all their opposition by becoming the party of provincial sovereignty in the new strong regional provinces which alone hold out the promise of fulfilling Canada's destiny?

The Liberal Party of Canada is in retreat. Losing every second round of federal by-elections, they have also been closed out of power in all of the provincial legislatures except Nova Scotia and Prince Edward Island. It is possible that five or ten years from now there will not be a single Liberal government in Canada, neither federal nor provincial, unless there is a major re-orientation of policy. The Liberals seem to be able to re-direct their entire philosophy, even without changing leaders sometimes. One of the most interesting questions of the next decade of Canadian politics will be whether the Liberals can respond again to the will of the people, or whether they are so committed to their present course that they will drive themselves into final oblivion. Thus far, they seem inclined to defend the indefensible, upholding centralism to the very end. If they continue to do so we must ensure that it is the end of the liberal party rather than the end of Canada.

Meanwhile, Prime Minister Trudeau in "the Emperor's new clothes" goes around making lovely speeches in the United States and everywhere in this country except in Parliament. His talk of unity, harmony and love has no substance. No policies are announced that could accommodate the diversity of Canada. And no new programs are planned to combat the serious problems we have in the economy, the French fact, lack of opportunity in the Atlantic, powerlessness in the West, exploitation of the north, and so on.

I could predict, unless by a miracle everyone sees

naked Liberalism for what it is, that the Liberals will win over 200 seats in the next election. When the identical panic spread through Quebec in the second last provincial election the Liberals used it to advantage and won 102 of 110 seats. With that majority there was no excuse for not governing but since they had inadequate policies the Liberals failed and the Parti Quebecois had its opportunity to make its contribution. Time will tell whether or not that contribution will be adequate but the whole nation is now set to go through a parallel experience. The common denominator is that the Liberal Party used exploitation of the Canadian unity issue to cover its lack of appropriate policies and to catapult itself into unprecedented power. Just as in Quebec, so much power with so little valid policy will lead to a collapse. After winning a strong, massive majority the Liberal Party can be depended upon to collapse of its own weight unless it becomes radically transformed and responsible to Canada's needs. While the Trudeau Liberals are engaged in this folly invented by the Bourassa Liberals, those of us who see an alternative vision for Canada must bide our time and keep our powder dry. The future will present new opportunities to share the vision and new methods to get the message across.

13

COWARDICE IN THE CAPITAL

This is an invitation to our political leaders to rise to the challenge of these times. Almost any of them could do it but it remains to be seen whether any of them have the courage and the foresight. If they are all so out of touch with the needs of the people in every region, including the most basic of all needs...the need to experience sovereignty...then somebody had better begin to give them a promise of the fate that awaits them and the fate that awaits Canada. Do any of them dare suppose that Canada is not at a turning point and that the upheavals across our land have no significance? Do they imagine that the three or four major , political parties now have platforms and policies that are adequate for the times? Do they dream that all of this will go away and that there will be business as usual with no fundamental change in either the structure of Canada or the configurations of its political parties? This is a watershed era, which will have consequences as great as, say, the Depression. New political movements have already begun. A regional sovereignty group is already in control in Quebec and such groups are springing up all over the West. Will any of our present leaders or any of our present political parties prove adaptable enough to give new leadership for these times? It is not enough to mearly beat back the forces of Separatism and to try to keep everybody happy in the old kind of federalized Canada.

The Liberal Party could do it. It would not be necessary for Liberals to give up the richness of their multi-cultural ethic nor even to draw back from commitments to the wider world. Even continentalism could flourish once an essential commitment has been made to the ultimate sovereignty of the provinces. The basic question is clear. Do they continue in the same direction that they are now moving in with federalized centralism, bilingualism and big government policies that try to look after us all, or do they make a new fundamental commitment to regional sovereignty? Yet if regional sovereignty is basically a conservative position, but one that the Progressive Conservative Party of Canada does not have the courage to endorse, then why should the Liberals bother to grasp that initiative? It is what the people want and need, but federal politics have become too divorced from reality to respond to the opportunity.

The Progressive Conservatives are never so confused as when they seek to establish for themselves what they call "a more truly conservative position". Taking their cues from the right wing of the American Republican Party, they then begin to confuse conservatism with reactionary views. One would think they might get a clue from the use of the word conservation by environmental groups, water resource people, recreation concerns, lobster fishermen and duck hunters. The conservation ethic that is demanded in an era of depleting resources and high priced energy is an ethic that simply calls us to a more human lifestyle.

The programs that respond to these needs cannot be initiated by Ottawa nor even administered by a federal bureaucracy. Community groups show that we, the people, have the greatest interest in the environment, dam construction and consumer protection. The best defence against the growing power of multinational corporations in Canada is not to give the federal government increased policing and watchdog ability but to increase the viability of the small business people in every part of the country. The way to get ourselves out of labor strikes that so hamper our economy is not to enable big business to finally beat back the outrageous demands of big labor but to find a way for those who invest capital and those who invest labor to manage their affairs together.

That too must be done essentially at the local level and only the provincial or regional governments will be in any kind of a position to encourage that development. The Progressive Conservative Party of Canada has a program calling out to it from the Canadian people. They may win a future federal election just because the Liberals seemed to have lost their way temporarily . But whether the Conservative Party will adopt policies that will enable us to conserve Canada and enable the people to keep sovereignty in their own hands remains to be seen. If they fail again they might as well be told now that this time they have contributed to the collapse of Canada.

Both Social Credit and the New Democratic Party have the possibilities of playing a creative role in the building of a new Canada or of dropping out of sight altogether. Of course, if they fail and if both the Liberals and the Conservatives fail, it may be Canada that drops out of sight altogether. The strangest scenario of all would be the formation of a popular front by the New Democrats and the Social Credit people.

The thought is immediately an affront to both of them. But even in their origins during the Depression they had something in common in the kind of populism that sought to help ordinary people in their desperate need. It is time for a new vision in Canada but before they can share in the new vision, these two splinter parties will find it necessary to drop their labels and slogans and jargon.

The New Democratic Party must get over its romantic attachment to Socialist language and Social Credit has to assure us that Fascism and "funny money" are gone forever. To a large extent both these parties have already begun to think creatively and to escape the confines of the past. In its opposition to the multinationals, the New Democratic Party must become committed to the small businessman as well as the family farm. If we are going to have laws against price-fixing by business we must also oppose wage-fixing by unions. That would not be hard for Social Credit to swallow, though it must begin to think more sincerely about co-management of industry. Both would be eager to scrap the ineffective welter of welfare measures in favor of a negative income tax or a guaranteed annual income. Most important of all, the Creditistes in Quebec, Alberta and British Columbia, along with the Socialists in Saskatchewan, Manitoba, Ontario and Cape Breton have a commitment to local concerns in a way that makes them perhaps most amenable to the kind of regional sovereignty that people everywhere in the world are craving in this new age.

On the other hand, given the improbability of such an alliance, a couple of other options remain open to the two smaller parties. Each of them has the possibility of recovering from its own weakness by the strong endorsement of new provincial sovereignty. Conceivably one of these parties could almost sweep the country on a platform of saving Canada in a new form of sovereign union. The fact is that almost any combination of events could bring about a change in a positive direction. So far nothing new is happening and no creative leadership is coming from Ottawa.

The first of several dangers we all face in federal politics is that absolutely nothing will happen and Canada will simply disintegrate. The second great danger is that somebody will come up with half a solution. Without courageously adopting a clear position that will bring new life to each of Canada's regions, the federal Conservatives could make an unspoken deal with the Parti Quebecois.

Quebec could establish a new arrangement with Canada whereby we exist together in some kind of association in which Quebecers have all the benefits of sovereignty but English Canada is still under a federal system. Quebec then surges forward to a new destiny of its own choosing while the only real development in English Canada is the construction of more office towers in Ottawa to house the still increasing bureaucracy. The rest of the country then truly disintegrates in frustration and Canada goes down the drain.

In the attempt to invite our present leaders and parties to take the initiative, the only Canadian politician we have ignored is Rene Levesque. He stands at center stage at present, as can be seen in program after newscast and page after page in the media. Most Canadians have begun to recognize the Parti Quebecois government as no group of radicals, but simply a center-left government committed first of all to clean government, honesty and integrity and secondly dedicated to ultimate sovereignty for Quebec. The confrontation politics now endorsed by the four federal parties will contribute nothing but grief to the future of Canada.

I wish to invite Mr. Levesque to undertake one simple act of leadership which can have positive repercussions throughout Canada. Let the Parti Quebecois word a referendum for the people of Quebec in such a way that, should the referendum pass, an identical referendum could be put to the rest of the country. Such a referendum might give a clear choice between "Quebec remaining as it is in a federal Canada" or "Sovereign Quebec proposing a new partnership with other sovereign regions of Canada". If it should happen that the referendum passes and the rest of the country spurns the initiative toward a new Canada of Sovereign Provinces then the next step for Quebec would be obvious and would be accepted by the rest of the country with only a sigh of regret.

If there is no clear platform from one or more of the federal parties committed to a Canadian Union of new Sovereign Provinces, then the initiative must pass to regional and provincial leaders, possibly including some of the strong provincial politicians such as Premier Bennett or Premier Lougheed in the region in which I live. Unilateral leadership on the part of provincial or regional groups might begin by an initial commitment to Canada, by which we mean a Canada that has room for a sovereign Quebec. But what we offer to Quebec, we must claim for ourselves.

One way remains to deal with federal politicians who lack courage and vision. Some of the separatist groups across the country are left-leaning, such as the Parti Quebecois in Quebec. Some of these separatist groups in the country are right wing groups, such as the Committee for Western Independence.

These labels and lines of distinction have become blurred in the crisis of the modern age, namely that people need to regain sovereignty for themselves. This whole spectrum of groups could now make common cause. A campaign to ensure that less than fifty per cent of the voters actually cast ballots in a future federal election could be the most effective way of illustrating to federal leaders that the people of Canada are seeking a new and better destiny. Voter apathy combined with strong leadership from the Parti Quebecois in its province and the various separatist groups in the West could produce a parliament that has the support of less than fifty per cent of Canadians and therefore no mandate whatsoever. The only problem is that the main beneficiary of such a boycott would be the Liberal Party whose supporters could then easily re-elect the Liberals who would continue to claim vindication of their policies.

At the present time I am not prepared to vote for any federal political party in Canada. I am not so fed up with the Liberal commitment to bigness in government that I am going to vote for the party of big business or the party of big unions. If it is time for a change from the Liberals, there is at present nobody standing as the kind of sovereign alternative that would give Canada a new future. By their policies of over centralization it is the federal politicians and bureaucrats who have got us into the problem that Canada now faces.

Now they ask for our continued goodwill and a mandate for them to get us out of the mess. Unless either the Liberals or the Conservatives or one of the other parties charts a new course responsive to the needs of human beings in the kind of world we live in, we should give them a clear message that we will get ourselves out of this predicament. In essence that is the clear message that the voters of Quebec have given in the context of their province. The dramatic impact of a federal election in which less than fifty per cent of the voters cast ballots would be a vote of no confidence in the kind of federalism, bureaucracy, and impersonal irresponsibility that has brought frustration to Canadian workers, businessmen, pensioners and unemployed and holds so little promise for our children.

14

THE PEOPLE OF CANADA

Federal politics are in a great deal of turmoil in Canada these days. But Canada itself is remarkably serene in the midst of the most important period of adjustment since Confederation. In spite of the sluggish economy brought on by the impossibility of federal solutions to our diverse problems, and in spite of the leadership vacuum in Ottawa, Canadians are finding sources of strength and wisdom within themselves and from other leaders. It is more than interesting that the strongest political leaders in the country have opted for provincial politics in the last decade. There seems to be little question that either Premier E. Schreyer of Manitoba or Premier D. Barrett of British Columbia could have won the leadership of the New Democratic Party a couple of years ago. Likewise in the Progressive Party, had either Premier Lougheed or Premier Davis stepped forward, not only would one of them have taken the leadership but the next election would go to the Conservatives not by default but by choice. As for Social Credit, if there had been an interest in federal politics, Premier Bennett of British Columbia could easily have taken the leadership position. However during the federal Social Credit convention, Bill Bennett was on a holiday in Hawaii.

Surely it is not that these men lack ambition. Moreover, politicians are not generally known for their humility and so we may imagine that had one of them taken the leadership of a federal party, he would not find it difficult to picture himself as the Prime Minister of Canada. Could it simply be that provincial politics is where the action is, in spite of the partial sovereignty that these provinces have at present?

It could even be that these best of our political leaders do care about the people and wish to respond to the actual needs of their regions. Municipal politics have also drawn strong leaders in recent times, from David Crombie in Toronto to Rod Sykes in Calgary. They are in double jeopardy, so to speak, because of the necessity for them to deal with two senior governments. They should be prepared to support regional sovereignty more than anyone else as a way of bringing accountability and resources for living closer to hand.

Media people sometimes have a good deal of difficulty in understanding why these people spurn federal politics. But it is of interest that even as decentralization grows, the media are catching the spirit and seeing the vision of a new Canada. Until very recently the hallmark of Canadian drama has been the lack of heroes.

It was as if we could not believe in ourselves sufficiently to imagine that there are Canadians who are fearless and determined. The only "John Wayne" who ever grew up in Canada, Lorne Greene, found it necessary to play out his part in the United States. Even on the comedy scene, it was satire that we depended upon, a la Wayne and Shuster. As valuable as it was, it displayed none of the self confidence of situation comedies such as the Mary Tyler Moore productions that we have imported so eagerly. That seems to have changed now. We not only have the King of Kensington to laugh at but also western heroes of our very own.

The dramatic series "Here To Stay" told the stories of people who came to this country not in simple poverty (for that is an American story) but people who came to this country out of actual defeat in Lithuania, Poland, the Ukraine, or Germany. They came here to stay. With all the courage and verve in the world they built new lives for themselves and contributed to Canada. The series "For The Record" not only tells about people as they really are, and the saga of building up the human community in Canada, but more than that, the media itself becomes heroic. The CBC has always excelled in documentaries and it is pure brilliance to apply those documentary techniques to dramatic situations in presenting modern issues. The program "Someday Soon" which projected us ahead to the year 1980, presents the crisis in southern Manitoba following the opening of the Garrison Dam in North Dakota. The farmland was flooded. Since that part of Canada often experiences floods there was no panic at first until they realized that the dam was diverting unprecedented levels of water and was going to continue to do so for some time. The diverted water came through barren lands that were extremely saline and the salt brought northward was about to do permanent damage to the fertile farmlands of southern Manitoba.

The CBC documentary style gave us every confidence that the facts were being adequately presented. The respect of the farmers for law and order, and their down-to-earth style as a way of life was realistically portrayed. Yet to our amazement the heroic element came to the fore as it was needed. In spite of the rage of the district councilman and the RCMP, these farmers took their own machinery and attempted to change the drainage patterns on provincial roadways. Never to be buffaloed by a cabinet minister they frankly and correctly assessed the do-nothing intentions of government.

I could tell you from long years of pastoring in western rural communities that there is almost nothing beyond the capability of these people, either in terms of planning or action.

After a preliminary visit to the dam site to check their facts, six of these farmers said goodbye to their families and at dawn one morning crossed the border into North Dakota. They jumped the wires on some huge American earth movers, and began to fill in the main channel from the dam. Strong and sincere and also worldly wise, they had left instructions for their families to phone one of the national television networks in Canada at about the time the action was to start. The networks contacted the politicians and the protest had international coverage at the highest level at the very moment the men were arrested.

These were no wild-eyed radicals looking for a cause. These were the toughest, smartest hombres in the world. They had a point to make and they knew how to make it. The issue was no trifling incident but reflects the growing concern of our times for food production and preservation of the environment, issues in conflict with the growing need for energy from dams and other sources.

"Someday Soon" should be seen again and again north and south of the border. It reflects the new maturity of the media come of age in Canada. There are great stories in Toronto and in southern Ontario and in the oceans and among the mountains. The dramatic episodes now unfolding in the North can be handled by the Canadian media, because producers and viewers have begun to believe in themselves. In spite of the allegations of Liberal politicians, and regardless of the CRTC Inquiry, these programs have won a respect for the CBC in Western Canada not equalled in history. There has been a genuine attempt at regionalization in the CBC under the present administration of the corporation. The positive results are but a preview of what to hope for in a regionalized Canada.

Many Canadians have recently become concerned about what appears to be the growth of racist sentiment in Canada. This is not Northern Ireland. It is not South Africa. And it is not the Middle East.

We are not going to have racial tensions get out of hand between French and English in Canada, nor are we going to allow the same thing to develop between native and white. The potential for danger is there, but we are absolutely determined not to let racism ruin this country anymore than outmoded political systems or economic theories. At the very beginning Canada was of course 100 per cent non-white but the immigrants came century upon century and have made it their home.

At first the Scots were not sure they wanted Irish in this country. Many years later the British elements here and there were not sure they wanted Eastern Europeans here and there have been pressures from large numbers of Italians in the East and Orientals in the West. But all these people have enriched Canada immeasurably and are now an accepted part of the fabric of our society.

More recent waves of immigrants have been from English speaking parts of the world, notably the United States of America, West Indies and other parts of the Commonwealth. The notable distinction in this case has been color, yet the integration proceeds. These people too, are making their contribution to fields such as education, medicine and music as well as labor. Such people bring brilliance and diversity to our land and make it a more truly human place.

Per capita, Canada now has a non-white population nearly as large as the United States. Once a problem was entrenched there, it took the Americans hundreds of years to begin to find a constructive solution. All mankind rejoices that the American people have taken steps to work through their problems now and have begun to resume a place of leadership in a very mixed world. This is one problem that Canada wishes to nip in the bud, for as other parts of the world have learned, no reactionary or repressive measures can succeed. Indeed the only way for us to avoid the bloodshed and turmoil that others have seen is to become colorblind.

There may be practical limitations to the total number of immigrants that Canada can absorb or even the number of students from abroad we can handle in any particular college. But as soon as race becomes either the basis of quota or unspoken guidelines for admission, Canada's bright future is finished. The Canada of great resources, splendid scenery and resilient environment , and the Canada of history and adventure and faith, can become the Canada of destiny only if our people remain pure in these most important respects.

By purity in Canada we don't mean purely Anglo Saxon, high caste Indian, black untainted by white or white untainted by black, but purely human. Purity in this country on the racial issue means that our spirit remains pure and free from racist bigotry and that is important for natives, Italians, English, French and all Canadians.

Canada is a multicultured society. That fact is only

accentuated by the reality that there are two large language areas. Other cultures are also valued but 200,000 or so Ukrainians just cannot make a language case for themselves that 5,000,000 or 6,000,000 French can. It is not even a simple question of which language you do prefer if you are French or English speaking at present. It is a hard question of practical realities. But let no one be misled that the establishment of a new Quebec is the establishment of a racial society.

Everything we know about the Parti Quebecois leadership disputes that. I first met Rene Levesque when he was a champion of English speaking students in Montreal, who were under pressure because their universities were losing grant money over the language issue. Peter Desbarats, in the book *Rene, a Canadian in Search of a Country*, gives us Premier Levesque's personal background and he shows that the new Premier is very much in favor of close relations with the rest of Canada, Europe and most especially the United States of America. Moreover, press reports have given us to understand that the present P.Q. cabinet is even more fluently bilingual than the former Liberal cabinet of the province of Quebec.

These people are of diverse cultural roots themselves, no simple collection of provincial habitants. Yet all have recognized that it is their region, their province, that offers them the only vehicle for sovereignty in the complex world in which we live. They and their forefathers have made a commitment, and they are better for it.

Canada is now and will always remain a multicultural nation. As for the language and cultural issue it must simply be recognized that within that potential sovereign region the majority must have a certain precedence. That is democracy and we applaud that kind of community adjustment wherever else we see it.

In the city of Dawson Creek, British Columbia, the mayor is of Norwegian ancestry. In the present bilingualism-biculturalism debate we would regard him as an English Canadian. That is the only language that he speaks. Both he and his forbears have made an adjustment to the community, the province and the region in which they made their home. Many Canadians were interested to find a Premier of Quebec a few years ago with the name of Daniel Johnson. In some quarters there was even surprise that an "English Canadian" would be elected Premier of that province.

Their amused surprise disappeared when they heard him speak and realized that he was only just learning English. French is the language of the sovereign people of Quebec and those immigrants from all parts of the world who have graciously adapted themselves are now totally integrated. There are French speaking clergy and elders of the United Church who are members and supporters of the Parti Quebecois. I was even somewhat surprised myself some months ago when I met some familiar sounding names as I began to have some dealings with Mr. Levesque's party people.

We were preparing for the release of the book *Separatism* and so I was introduced to the press secretary of the Parti Quebecois, Mrs. O'Leary. She too has some difficulty with English but there is no question that she has adjusted to the community and province in which she lives and that the province is for her the vehicle for the sovereignty that she and every other modern person needs. The list could go on, with examples like Robert Burns, formerly the House Leader of the Parti Quebecois, and now one of the most senior cabinet ministers.

The Scottish poet that we all know was a man of the people and would be proud of his namesake in Quebec. The same point could no doubt be made regarding the

P.Q. Minister of Communications, Louis O'Neill, a new press secretary named McKay, and many others. The son of Daniel Johnson is a P.Q. representative and another of this Scottish-Irish clan. Regardless of origins, these people are now Quebecois and they are fully immersed in the culture of their province. There are parallels in the West and in other regions also.

But what of the Mackaseys and Bronffmans? The former Liberal cabinet minister and the head of the distillery industry seem to have something against putting sovereignty in the hands of the people. That is where sovereignty belongs and sovereignty exercises its own influence to make governments responsible. The Parti Quebecois originally intended to proceed with nationalization of various industries but found that it was local Quebec businessmen who would be hurt most. The government at Quebec City can feel that pressure in a way that the federal government cannot. Nationalization plans are now in abeyance, for the more sovereignty is placed in the hands of the people the fewer mistakes are made because of the unrealistic idealism of bureaucratic experts or the pipe dreams of politicians.

In the new Canada we will require some form of constitution, perhaps even an adaptation of the British North America Act. It might be more productive to simply begin together afresh but one of the dangers is the assumption that whatever constitution is written should last forever. That has never been true anywhere in the world, for throughout history constitutions have had durability of only a few hundred years at the most. The constitutions that have lasted long have been in fact so vague that they have been interpreted differently from age to age.

It was that kind of flexibility that enabled America, nearly 200 years after the writing of the constitution, to reinterpret it to include black Americans as voting citizens. It is the same kind of constitutional flexibility that has enabled the British Parliament to undergo vast reforms. We need that kind of flexibility in Canada and perhaps an ideal way to begin is to recognise the limitations of any constitution. A novel idea would be to commit ourselves to a constitution for a limited time, such as 100 years.

As Canada moves into a new phase as a Union of Sovereign Provinces, let us simply invite the province of Quebec to join with the rest of us for another 100 years. It is true that Sovereign Provinces would have the ultimate right of withdrawal from any union but that right cannot be used as a threat in negotiatons over specific issues and that right cannot be exploited politically in every single provincial election.

Dates are valuable for the establishment of both goals in the future and mileposts in history. I take 1497 for the claiming of Newfoundland, 1670 for the establishment of Rupertsland as the prairie region and 1793 for the beginning of the mountain region. Those are the dates of specific actions that make each of these three regions into united entities and the bases of Sovereign Provinces, now that the people have come of age. Despite the fact that our original confederation has turned into a federation we can still treasure the date on which Canada as a whole came into being. July 1, 1867, was the day of Confederation and we mark it now as Canada Day.

If we can straighten out this confederation or federation problem, Canada Day may be celebrated by Quebecers in the future with the same historic sense as the rest of Canada. As the next centennial of confederation, the year 2076 would commend itself as the time when the constitution will be reviewed again and each of the Sovereign Provinces is given an opportunity to assess its commitment to the Canadian Union. At that time Quebec or any other Province could choose to opt out of the Union or to commit itself to another 100 years. The latter prospect should appear all the more attractive as the years go by.

I would propose that each of the sovereign regions of Canada be given the choice now of opting in or opting out with the understanding that if it's in, then we remain together for nearly another century at least, until 2067. It must be understood of course that all throughout that time sovereignty rests in the hands of the people and is primarily exercised through their strong provincial governments. That form of constitution should set the style for all manner of co-operative efforts in Canadian life.

Groups such as the credit unions and the caisse populaires may now seize the initiative in fashioning the new Sovereign Union of Canada. The credit unions already operate on the basic premise that the ultimate power resides with the members. To use that specific example again, the British Columbia Central Credit Union has nothing to fear from a Canadian Central office because power runs backwards as compared with the federalistic model. As a matter of exciting precedence, the Central Credit Unions of other provinces could indicate their faith in this way of doing things and their goodwill toward the province of Quebec by offering to establish the offices of Canadian Central in Montreal.

The Caisse Populaires of Quebec have recently opened a huge skyscraper headquarters in Montreal. Surely a desk could be found as the paper work center for the pooling of assets which will give credit unions access to the kind of electronic and computer services that are now required on a cross-Canada basis. The time has come for Canadians, in whatever organizations they belong to, to insist upon sovereignty for their provinces. It is not always possible to bring final control back to the local community level but it must be brought back at least to a level where it is accessible and at the same time strong enough to be functional. Then we can establish new con-federal links.

The lingering fear will remain in the minds of some that even these provinces are not strong enough or sufficiently populous to be sovereign. True, this is an age of interdependency and when it comes right down to it there is a question about the sovereignty of any nation, state or province in the world these days. But it is interesting to note in passing that the population of all four provinces which originally made up Canada was just more than 2,000,000 in the year 1867. That is, the population today of Atlantic Canada that includes Newfoundland and Labrador, Nova Scotia, most of New Brunswick, Prince Edward Island and Cape Breton. That is also the population of a modern Rupertsland given Manitoba, Saskatchewan and the Eastern Arctic.

In 1867 nothing was certain but that Canadians were setting off on a grand adventure. There were risks that they faced but they banded together because none of those tiny colonies had anything like sovereign ability at the time. One thing they had, though, was faith in themselves. We should like to think that we are worthy of the faith they had in us as well. As they believed in themselves and established structures that were appropriate for their needs, we must believe in ourselves and face the issues of our time.

It is time to realize that we can do so as Canadians and that there is a way for both French Canadians and English Canadians, regardless of their origins, to evolve a new future for Canada. It is not necessary to cut our roots with the past, for Cabot and Champlain, Radisson and Groseilliers belong to all of us. So do the bones of Henry Hudson and the trails of Alexander Mackenzie.

But Rupertsland did not remain the possession of the Hudson's Bay Company forever. New France had its day and no Quebecers want to return to that era. Atlantic Canada had a time when it flourished but though times have changed life can flourish there again. We cannot remain camped on Mackenzie's trails forever; the promise of the region he established must be fulfilled.

I have proposed elsewhere that a Canada come-of-age can take a new role of leadership in the old Commonwealth of Nations. These mighty Sovereign Provinces, in a union with one another, might also be ready to go into business with the others on this continent with whom we share many interests. And if one Province wishes special ties with French nations why should the others object? As a youth, Canada was shy. We are not an aggressive people but we have reached our maturity now and in the determined confidence shown by the people in "Someday Soon", we shall claim the twentieth century for Canada.

15

THE SOVEREIGNTY-ASSOCIATION MOVEMENT

The Parti Quebecois which now forms the government of Quebec is an outgrowth of the Mouvement Souverainete-Association. The movement has never been in favor of the kind of radical separation between Quebec and the rest of Canada that would make us two countries as separate as the United States and Mexico, for example. From the very begining, there has been the notion of "sovereignty" but always in "association" with other sovereign Canadians. A strong measure of political independence and the right to set economic policy as well as cultural autonomy is desired, but from the beginnings of the movement in 1967, there has been a commitment to a wider association or union with the remainder of Canada if all parties are willing.

It is unnecessary and wrong for Westerners or anybody else to speak of total separation of their region when even Rene Levesque, in a speech on the French TVA television network, March 13, 1977, affirmed that for Quebec to gain the independence it needs, it may not be necessary to break up Canada. He was speaking in support of his Economic Development Minister Bertrand Landry and Parti Quebecois back bencher Gerald Godin who have both said publicly that the P.Q. considers separation not a goal in itself, but an instrument to achieve social and economic goals. If the latter can be attained within some new Canadian structure, such would be the basis of the new confederation. Gerald Godin has said on English television:

"If we can get what we want without fracturing Confederation we will try to do so."

Bernard Landry was addressing a group of Winnipeg businessmen when he said that Quebec did not want to "harm" Canada or fracture "the whole". He went on to say that:

"If you find yourself out in a boat when a storm comes up, even if you are nearly freezing you don't build a fire in the boat."

There can be little question that Quebecers want fundamental changes in the way that the ship of state is sailed. To press the metaphor a little further, in our own lifetime we have seen the unionization of seamen and we have seen the navy taken over in an integration of armed forces. Perhaps on the wider issue it is changes of this magnitude that are desired rather than the sinking of the ship. In support of the more moderate of his ministers, Mr. Levesque himself said:

"We never said that by political sovereignty—that is, the right of Quebec to govern itself freely, like any normal people—we never said that meant the break-up of Canada.

"We always talked about an association. We always talked about the new ties being formed in Europe and all over the world. There is no reason why what might be called a renewal of Canadian structures would not, at once, aid the cause of a healthy Canada and the liberty of Quebec."

The time is right for politicians and others in the regions and provinces to begin a listening part of the dialogue, for Mr. Trudeau himself has ruled out the possibility of a future association between autonomous parts of Canada. Until this issue is clarified it is too soon for Western Separatists to talk of outright secession.

The slogan of the Western National Party, in Alberta, is appropriate: "Separation if necessary, but not necessarily separation." There is value in their organizing, to be prepared for the future in the event that Quebec does pull out of Canada altogether. In the meanwhile, Western separatist groups would do us all a service if they were able to organize together into a Sovereign Association Movement.

The value of a Sovereign Association Movement is obvious. Such a movement will help us to clarify the issues and define some of the objectives of Western autonomy either within a new confederation or in an undetermined future. It is important now for Westerners to get their act together, regardless of what goes on in the remainder of the country.

For the two far western provinces and the north-west, the Mountain Region or "Mackenzieland", there are some real parallels with the development of the Sovereignty Association Movement in Quebec. That movement was made up of a variety of separatists and independent groups who bridged their differences and made common cause for the sake of their region. They came together to form the Mouvement Souverainete--Association.

We have the Committee for Western Independence and the Western Canada Party in British Columbia. We have the Independent Alberta Association and the Western National Party in Alberta as well as the Dene nation, the Metis Association in the Northwest

Territories, COPE in the Western Arctic Islands and various independent groups in the Yukon. An umbrella organization to unite these groups in a common movement for autonomy in the mountain region could have future benefits regardless of developments elsewhere. It is obvious to all that small provinces cannot play ball in the same league as Quebec and Ontario. The object of coming together to form a sovereign province is not an attempt to beat Quebec and Ontario at their own game. What is desired is a greater measure of equality between the regions which can then ensure either a better future for us within Canada or the outline of our future in the event of the break up of Canada.

In the event that Quebec is able to work things out with the rest of Canada and gain for itself the desired measure of autonomy, there is no way that the other regions, whether Atlantic or Western, would want to continue without a similar measure of autonomy. We must ensure that whatever measure of sovereignty Quebec gets, we also have the opportunity to attain.

This is not such a radical proposal and may eventually be seen as a normal and healthy part of the evolution of a new Canada. Between them, the four outright separatist groups, the Committee for Western Independence, the Western Canada Party, the Western National Party, and the Independent Alberta Party, the Western National Party, and the Independent Alberta Association represent approximately 10,000 members. The movement is small at present, roughly equal to the movement in Quebec at a similar stage of development, a dozen years ago.

If the Western Canada Party runs candidates in the next British Columbia provincial election, and the Western National Party runs a full slate in Alberta, they might poll a tiny seven per cent of the votes. That was the figure that such groups attained in Quebec just before coming together as one political force with a viable platform.

Following the example of the successful movement in Quebec, those concerned for Western sovereignty must maintain their contact with those who are active in traditional political parties. The traditional parties are understandably nervous of any new trend, for reasons we have already considered. However, individual members of traditional parties, including some sitting members of the provincial or federal parliaments, might well be attracted to the sovereignty movement once the movement jells. The "Rene Levesque" of Western Canada is possibly sitting in a provincial legislature or the Federal House at this very moment.

The Movement should be open to individuals from traditional political parties as well as from the two new Western Independence parties and other groups. I personally know members of the Western legislatures and federal parliament from three parties...Social Credit, New Democrat and Conservative...who are fundamentally sympathetic to Western autonomy. Those who are members of established parties can work to have the concept of sovereign-association accepted by whatever parties they belong to as the basis of a new Confederation. Premier Levesque first attempted to have sovereignty adopted as a policy of the Quebec Liberal Party when he was a member and cabinet minister. Such an attempt within the ranks of an established party today might meet with more ready acceptance, given the events of the last few years in Canada and Quebec.

It is the Conservative Party in Ottawa that has shown the only glimmer of understanding of the need and the reasons for decentralization. The Leader of the

Opposition, Mr. J. Clark, has indicated that a Progressive Conservative government would make a complete return of health, welfare, education and some other fields to the provinces. The trouble with such a simple policy is that it fails to recognize the basic reason why creeping centralism sneaked up on us in the first place—eight of the ten provinces are too small to undertake such responsibilities.

The concept is good and as the original party of con-federation the Tories should be the natural defenders of provincial rights. Before such a policy can be effective in a new Confederation there must be more than a token effort at making each of the "provinces" large enough and sufficiently viable for these increased responsibilities. This is the first task of the Sovereignty-Association Movement in the Western regions and in Atlantic Canada.

It will take a decade of growth and organization, but regional or provincial sovereignty is an idea for which the time has come in a Canada-come-of-age. We do have too much geography and too much diversity to be governed as a centralized federation. Canadians everywhere are looking for a new alternative whereby this most bounteous land in the world may hold together and realize its potential. Both Quebec and Ontario are already suitably organized for the new confederation. To make it happen, all that is required is for one of the other regions to organize. If Mackenzie-land can seize the initiative; that is to say, if it appears to those in other small provinces that Alberta and British Columbia are moving together toward a new kind of province, equal to Quebec and Ontario, that will be the impetus for similar movements to come forth in Atlantic Canada and in Rupertsland.

It is too late to turn back the clock. The status quo of federalism in Canada was dealt the mortal blow on

November 15, 1976. Canada will never be the same again but it is up to all of us to decide whether or not all Canada can go forward to a new and better future. It is not a case of "what if" Quebec wants a new form of association. The only question is "what kind of association shall we have?"

If all Quebec wants is an economic association called Canada, that may be acceptable to Westerners. There are some who would say that is all Canada was ever intended to be. If Quebec and the others want something more...joint defense and "common front" foreign policy ...then Canada can continue in such mutually advantageous endeavors. Westerners are open to negotiations in regard to various forms of association, but this time we too insist on negotiating as equals. We too are deserving and ready for sovereignty. We would be almost unanimous that Canada should continue in some new form but not even Les Quebecois feel stronger than we do about the failure of federalism. We cannot go back to the way we were. If we must create something new on the face of the earth then we have good reason to go forward together as Canadians.

16

BLUEPRINT FOR A BETTER CANADA

There are so many ways in which Canada can be improved. In many instances it was haphazard planning for developments of other countries that account for the way in which this country is organized today. The best example of the need for reorganization is the way in which the country is now designed around an East-West flow of goods and people. That development was made intentionally with the border between Canada and her only physical neighbor who happens to be stronger in many respects and therefore able to engage us in economic activity and mutual stimulation. That development was, of course, enhanced by the pattern of railroad building in a previous century. Yet virtually all sociologists, economists, and geographers are unanimous in the opinion that a more natural flow of activity is North and South, in any part of North America.

Canada occupies more than half of the North American continent and should be free to organize again along more sensible lines. Now that the whole country is well developed, or nearly so, the rationale for organizing the five sovereign regions as I attempted to outline becomes apparent. It is certainly true that in each of the five regions there is a different culture (if culture may simply be defined as lifestyle) as well as a different economy. No part of Canada is a "have-not" region. It is just that some regions have suffered more under federalism. To organize each region with considerable autonomy on a North-South basis is one of the steps necessary to enable each of the regions to come into its own. There have been some historical precedents for such a development as, for example, when Manitoba began its northern expansion or when both Quebec and Ontario grew from their tiny size along the St. Lawrence and Great Lakes to eventually include everything to the north of the Canadian mainland.

In the new Canada it will be possible for both Quebec and Ontario to take a more responsible attitude toward the northern parts of those great provinces. Likewise, in the West we shall give our own North an opportunity to develop in tandem with the southern parts of the Prairie region and the Mountain region. For the North to develop on its own would be a promise of the frustration and alienation that other provinces have experienced. The Atlantic region will be more free to develop its natural markets with the Eastern seaboard of the United States and Newfoundland will get maritime support for development.

All Canada will flourish, sharing in joint activities through our national capital Ottawa—in those matters that we choose—but with far greater autonomy in terms of our own lifestyle and development within our regions. What holds many people back from this view is the fear that strengthening the regions will weaken Canada. The opposite is true, for when the five strong regions come into their own all Canada will be strong, whereas at present, there are many regions that lag behind.

Apparently those regions that prosper can do little for the others in the federal system. Canada is weak now in the sense that any chain is as weak as its weakest link. The weak links of Canada are caused by the economy in the Atlantic region, cultural concerns in Quebec and a sense of alienation from power in the West. And all of these things sap the strength of the country and deprive Canada of a proper sense of vitality and destiny. When we eliminate these problems we will find out from our history, and because of our present expediency, that there are many areas in which all Canadians will want to cooperate. Those will become the responsibility of the confederal capital and its smaller but important bureaucracy.

It seems strange indeed that when we begin to delineate those areas of confederal responsibility and to list out those aspects of our lives that will be under provincial jurisdiction that the lines of distinction fall pretty close to the original British North America Act. The hatred of federalism in the West and in Quebec ought not to deter us from the concept of Confederation, merely because in our history the original Confederation became a federation.

The confederal cabinet should consist of the Prime Minister, the President of the Privy Council, the Secretary of State and a number of other portfolios with important areas of jurisdiction. The Department of External Affairs would continue with its responsibility for foreign policy and passports. The Minister of Finance would have the important responsibility and the very difficult task of monitoring the common Canadian currency in its relationship with other monetary systems of the world.

There would of course be a minister of Canadian

Defense and a Postmaster General for Canada. The confederal parliament might continue its responsibility for Veteran Affairs, International Trade and there would quite possibly be the need of a Solicitor-General for Canada. All the other areas of the present federal government, which were originally given to the provinces, would be returned to the provinces. This is possible only when the provinces become sufficiently large and strong enough to fulfil their responsibilities.

The sovereign provinces would take from the present federal government responsibility for Industry, for Labor, Transport, Energy, Mines and Resources, Agriculture, Science and Technology, Urban Affairs, Communications, Health and Welfare, Public Works, Manpower and Immigration, Small Business and Recreation. Make no mistake, the responsibilities that remain with our confederal capital, Ottawa, are major and essential. When the provinces come into their own then Quebec, the West and all Canada will be content to leave important functions to Ottawa. Even the process of defining these functions may not prove so difficult once they are narrowed down and limited to certain spheres.

This is not a radical position. What I have described is a true confederation. How ironic that only the Province of Quebec seems to have maintained the spirit of the British North America Act, as it has done by insisting on its own powers in fields of Communication, Health, Welfare, and so on. It could be argued that only Quebec is in step with the BNA Act and that the other nine provinces and the federal government are all out of step.

As might be expected, since this country is most suitably organized as a confederation, once we get things back into proper perspective a lot of our other problems will be solved as well. A critical problem in Canada is the economy. One of the reasons for the problem of inflation is the excessive amount of government for a country with so small a population. Each of the areas that the federal government have taken away from the provinces has resulted in duplication of services. The provinces have maintained departments in all the appropriate fields but they have been ineffective departments. To remove so many areas from the fedeal jurisdiction and return them to the provinces will result in a drop in costs. True, provincial costs will go up but ٦ot to the extent that we have in a system whereby two levels of government attempt to do the same things. This drop in federal costs would be at least equal to the federal portion of income tax. This is one more area that the federal government has taken away from the provinces which could now be brought back into line. The disappearance of federal income tax would be a stimulation to the economy which should be taken as an historic opportunity to satisfy both the demands of labor and the requirements of industry. When each wage earner in Canada finds that his cheque has no more federal income tax deducted from it he will experience a major increase in purchasing power.

In the British Isles a major attempt to control inflation has been launched with a policy of large scale government tax cuts in response to a promise from the unions to hold wage increases to four per cent. This opportunity could be found in Canada also, by savings through implementing the simple principle that each department of government be assigned to either the confederal jurisdiction or the provincial jurisdiction, and that no department exists at both levels. Tax savings would be immense.

There are those who would maintain that we would simply exchange one bureaucracy for another. There are two answers to that. First, we already have two bureaucracies and to return to the provinces those powers originally given to then in the constitution is to simplify and streamline a system that has got out of hand through creeping federalism. Second, in terms of the sense of sovereignty, the bureaucracy of the sovereign regions is one that can be more easily controlled and changed by the people. We even know the names of the bureaucrats in our regions.

I recently found myself in conversation at an airport with one of British Columbia's senior advisers in agriculture. Martin Hunter is a member of my congregation but is frequently away attending to his duties as a member of that "super board". the regulating authority of all British Columbia's marketing boards. A couple of farmers came up to us and said to Martin, "Mr. Hunter, we need to get in touch with the Deputy Minister of Agriculture, Sig Pedersen. His home phone number must be unlisted but you know him socially, could you give us his phone number?" My friend was not sure if it was an unlisted number and so rather than give it, he simply went to the phone and dialled the number for the farmers who then spoke to the Deputy Minister. When Martin came back to me I said to him, "Lucky for them you knew his number. Would you be able to give them the number of the federal Deputy Minister?"

After a moment of consideration my friend replied that not only would he be unable to give the number, he did not even know the name of the federal Deputy Minister. Under the constitution, agriculture is a provincial matter and yet we all know that the federal minister and his department have the most authority. None of us knows who these people are, and we have no contact with them. Indians find this in the Department of Indian Affairs which spends so much money on its bureaucracy that if the whole thing were shut down every native Indian in Canada could be given an income of seven thousand dollars a year. From one department to another we see waste, re-duplication, lack of responsibility and no direct accountability to the people, whether they are businessmen, laborers, natives, farmers or anything else. Just as a federal inquiry found that the federal policy of bilingualism is not working, the Economic Council of Canada has declared that the Department of Regional Economic Expression has failed to alter regional disparities. The same body found that the present freight rate structures prevent the establishment of manufacturing industries in the West. The federal people need inquiries to find these things out but all the people in the regions know these things. CMHC is financing the future slums of Dawson Creek by enforcing grant scales made for Ontario. Here in the North concrete costs $50 per yard—the grant allows for $35 and so we build a Senior Citizens Lodge by putting in the cheapest materials elsewhere to make up for the over run on concrete. Enough! The examples could go on forever.

In the final analysis what is needed is a new and genuine Confederation. To be genuine the provinces must be viable. They must be autonomous and they must be ultimately sovereign. By viable, we mean that there will be no weak links in confederation in the sense that no province will be too small to fulfil its responsibilities. By autonomy we mean that each province must have both the resources and the authority to conduct its own affairs on a wide spectrum of activities. By sovereignty we mean that each province is given the opportunity to opt in by choice to common programs in a number of areas, especially defense, foreign affairs, currency union, postal services, and the like. There will be the ultimate possibility of a province's withdrawal from confederation but opting into a sovereign union century by century, in which all

154

the provinces invest some of their sovereignty in a central parliament by choice rather than by compulsion. The reasons for remaining together will be clearly apparent.

Perhaps the city in which I have had the greatest response to this approach is Edmonton. I have done a number of shows and interviews in practically all the radio and television stations. During one of the several interviews that I had over station CHED I was asked by Eddie Keen, "Where in the world is there an analogy for this kind of national arrangement? Has it worked anywhere else? And if not, why should we imagine that it would work in Canada?" My immediate response to him was that his question was all too-Canadian.

We cannot believe that we could do something new on the face of the earth. There is no other country like Canada anywhere in the world. Even the USSR, which is the only country of similar size, has failed to develop many of its regions because of the central authority of Moscow. True, there is a new attempt at harmony between distinctive regions in Europe, where many sovereign states are voluntarily cooperating to establish a common market, and a currency union with various other aspects of unity still to come. There will be a parliament of Europe but each of the regional parliaments will remain ulitmately sovereign—and so there is one analogy, but that is not the important thing. We in Canada must learn to believe in ourselves and if it means that we must do something new and different, let us have confidence in ourselves and in one another.

Perhaps a more important issue is the question of what happens if we fail. I see an ugly spectre of our own particular brand of racism ready to tear us apart. We pride ourselves that when Europe went through the agony of prejudice against Jews we were above all of that. Our record was not perfect but in Canada there has never been a strong anti-semitic movement or feeling. Certainly there are a few "kooks" but most of us are distressed when our Jewish population even imagines that it is a serious thing. For several generations we have had the luxury of standing to one side while the United States has gone through a period of racial confrontation.

Blacks in this country are not in a favored position but there has not been open racism and many of our community leaders are in fact Negro. Once again, there are a few "kooks" in the country but just as anti-semitism is somebody else's problem, so is the color problem, for the most part. But this spring there was a hockey game in Edmonton which showed the potential for a problem of another dimension. A team from Quebec was visiting the West as part of a "goodwill" attempt, with an opportunity for the young players to see the rest of Canada and learn to love it.

Apparently there is some age differential in the juvenile categories and so it developed that on this particular occasion, the Quebec players were matched against slightly older Westerners. By chance, as well, there was a noticeable size and weight differential between the two teams. It was obvious early in the first game that there was to be no real contest in terms of the outcome of the game. When the game finally ended (or, rather, was called off part-way through) the Alberta team was leading eleven to three. However, they were also leading in another category, having picked up twenty-two of the twenty-nine penalties up to that point in the game. The Westerners were getting a clear delight out of manhandling the French. The jeers from the stands of "Kill the frogs" were taken almost literally by the players. The boys from Quebec were outmatched in every way, though the role of French players in

156

professional hockey would be the proof that the event in Edmonton was merely a matter of circumstance. Stitched and bloody and frightened, the Quebecers came back on the ice period after period until early in the third period their coach pulled his team from the ice and they packed their bags. Those in the stands who were inciting the Alberta players and shouting the racial obscenities were not "kooks". They were ordinary businessmen and laborers, housewives and mothers. They mow their lawns, they support amateur sport and they go to church on Sundays. These are the kinds of people who were responsible for anti-semitism in Hitler's Germany and these are the kinds of people who are responsible for segregation in the United States and South Africa. The danger is very real.

The next day I heard one commentator in Edmonton express the hope that the newspapers in Montreal would forgive and forget and not make a big issue out of this incident. This is the same kind of spineless wailing that English Canadians have always offered to Quebec. When the White Paper on the French Language for Quebec was introduced by the Parti Quebecois the government of the Province of Ontario was distressed.

"Give us one more chance to prove that we will treat our French minority well in the Province of Ontario" was the kind of thing we were hearing. And so our politicians promise that we will all make a better effort at learning French but the people resist, for this is not the solution to the problems of our country. The direction in which our leaders are moving at present is responsible for fear and frustration, alienation and antagonism and unworthy emotions of a sort I never thought I would see in Canada.

We can give Quebec its sovereignty and invite a sovereign Quebec to share in a new Confederation of Sovereign Provinces. We have had it with federalism but we must act before the story of Canada becomes the story of Ulster, Lebanon or South Africa. What we are willing to give to Quebec we must also have for each of the Canadian regions. Canadians everywhere need neither federation nor separatism, but a true and genuine confederation.

At any rate this is the Western position: we want not separatism and not federalism but sovereignty. Sovereignty does not preclude cooperation, unity or harmony. The Western position is remarkably similar to that of Quebec. The time for action is near and the need for creative leadership is great. But it is not too late for Canada.

It is too late for federalism. It is too late for bilingualism. And it is too late for centralized economy and faceless bureaucracy.

But it is not too late for confederation.

We have all the reasons we need to work things out in a renewal of Canada as a true Confederation of Sovereign Provinces. *Let us do it.*

THE END

APPENDIX

SELECTIONS FROM CONSTITUTIONAL TRENDS
AND THE COST OF CONFEDERATION WESTERN
PREMIERS' TASK FORCE ON CONSTITUTIONAL
TRENDS
MAY 5th, 1977 BRANDON, MANITOBA

1. BACKGROUND

The Western Premiers' Conference, held in Medicine
Hat on April 28th, 1976, released a communique on
constitutional matters which read in part:

Concern was expressed by the Premiers with regard
to recent federal legislative moves into areas of provincial constitutional jurisdiction. Such moves include
federal legislation and proposals in areas such as:
securities, mutual funds, electronic payments systems; telecommunications and cable systems; as well
as certain areas of competition policy and consumer
protection.

It was agreed that these possible federal intrusions
called for a careful and coordinated analysis by the
western provinces.

2 FORMATION OF THE TASK FORCE

The Hon. K. Rafe Mair, Minister of Consumer & Cor-
prate Affairs for B.C. was appointed the Task Force
Chairman. The other members of the Ministerial Task
Force were the Hon. Lou Hyndman, Alberta Minister of
Federal and Intergovernmental Affairs, the Hon. Roy
Romanow, Saskatchewan Attorney-General and the
Hon. Ian Turnbull, Manitoba Minister of Consumer,
Corporate and Internal Services. Mr. Turnbull's
representation on the Task Force was recently assumed
by the Hon. Howard Pawley, Attorney-General for
Manitoba.

3. SCOPE OF THE INVESTIGATION

There was agreement to limit the work of the Task
Force to these areas at present:

1. Consumer & Corporate Affairs
2. Natural Resources
3. Housing and Urban Development
4. Economic Development
5. Communications
6. Immigration, Manpower and Labour
7. Administration of Justice
8. Federal Constitutional Litigation

The following areas of federal encroachment are widely recognized but are not covered in this report:

9. Finance
10. Human Resources
11. Education
12. Health

I. Consumer and Corporate Affairs

The Task Force expressed concern that proposed federal intrusions in the area of consumer and corporate affairs appeared to be a significant attempt to regulate most features of the credit-payment-financial institution system. They agreed that these national policies were often insensitive to provincial jurisdiction and priorities. The Task Force felt that although there was some merit to these federal proposals several concerns remained and they asked that a reassessment of federal-provincial relations in this area be made before these federal intrusions are proceeded with.

The Task Force made the following comments and recommendations:

1. The Borrower's and Depositor's Protection Act
The Task Force expressed concern that this legislation could lead to a considerable dislocation of provincial mortgage legislation, trade practices and consumer credit legislation. A national regulatory presence for all financial institutions (including retail credit grantors), provincial credit unions, and provincial treasury branches would also be established. As such, conflicting federal and

provincial legislation will exist and there is a very strong possibility that constitutional litigation will occur. The Task Force suggested that the whole question be reassessed in light of these realities, and that provincial representations requesting that no action be taken without further federal-provincial consultation should be submitted.

2. Competition Policy [Stage 2]

This bill will establish a National Markets Board to deal with numerous aspects of corporate market conduct. Provincial and local priorities could easily be disregarded in this comprehensive federal regulatory system. The Task Force expressed concern about the constitutionality of this policy. They suggested that the possibility of challenging this legislation's constitutionality should be explored by the province(s). Provincial and/or regional development should also be recognized as a factor in arriving at national policy decisions.

3. Bank Act 1977

The Task Force noted that the federal Bank Act, which requires membership in the Canadian Payments Association, would in fact govern the activities of all financial institutions in Canada, regardless of jurisdictional origin. As such, the Bank Act carries complicated implications for the provinces. A wide range of objections to this act were presented in the interprovincial brief of December 1976. The Task Force suggested follow-up to determine the adequacy of the federal response to provincial concerns.

4. Electronic Payments Systems

These proposals would establish a centralized electronic clearing mechanism for deposit-taking institutions. This system is of immediate concern to the provinces considering the impact it could have on communications systems, debtor-creditor relations, consumer credit, human rights and privacy, contracts and jurisdiction over provincial financial institutions. In light of provincial interest in continuing recent federal-provincial consultation on this matter, the Task Force recommended that better liaison between the two levels of government be sought.

5. Trade Practices

Concern was expressed that the federal government intends to develop its own Trade Practices Act, notwithstanding the presence of existing and proposed provincial legislation. As such, federal actions in this regard would create conflicting legislation and cause confusion for businesses and consumers. The provinces of British Columbia, Alberta and Saskatchewan asked the federal government to refrain from legislating in this area.

6. Bankruptcy Act

These proposals would create a broader base for federal involvement in debtor assistance programs which might erode or eliminate existing provincial programs. The Task Force suggested that firm assurances should be obtained from the federal government that provincial exemptions legislation will be recognized in respect of the Act's treatment of consumer debtors. Provinces wishing to operate or institute debtor counselling assistance programs should be delegated the necessary powers and should receive reasonable financial assistance for such operations.

7. Proposed Mutual Funds Act and Securities Act

Considering that provincial programs in these two areas have been operating effectively for some time the proposed federal legislation would create duplicative and conflicting regulations. A good case for this separate or additional level of federal regulations under either heading has not been made. The Task Force felt that there should be a reassessment of the proposed legislation in light of their concerns.

II Natural Resources

The Task Force agreed that some of the most contentious issues in federal-provincial relations in recent years have centered around the natural resource sector. Various federal initiatives, especially since the energy crisis in the fall of 1973, have resulted in increased tensions between the federal government and the provinces, and in some cases have severely restricted the freedom of provincial governments to exercise their responsibilities over the management of renewable and nonrenewable resources.

The Task Force outlined their concerns in these areas and made the following recommendations:

1. Renewable Resources

NATIONAL FORESTRY POLICY   Task Force acknowledged a need for national uniformity of forestry statistics and standards and recognized the importance of assessing the resource's financial benefits. But, because of the vagueness of the federal proposals and in view of possible jurisdictional problems, they felt that the objectives of the program should be more clearly outlined, perhaps via CCREM (Canada Council of Resource and Environment Ministers), in order that legitimate areas for federal involvement could be closely defined.

2. Nonrenewable resources

NONDEDUCTIBILITY OF OIL AND GAS ROYALTIES— Provinces of British Columbia, Alberta and Saskatchewan maintained that this provision was a serious challenge to the fundamental rights of the provinces to control and benefit from the development of the resources they own. Their reasoning stemmed from the effect the tax measure would have on a province's ability to tax its resources; the effects these tax measures would have on the petroleum industry, i.e. discouraging oil exploration activity and thus Canada's energy supplies; and the effects the policy would have on a provincial government's attempts to diversify economically.

PETROLEUM ADMINISTRATION ACT–The provinces of British Columbia, Alberta and Saskatchewan expressed reservations about Part 3 of the Petroleum Administration Act as it actually amounts to an assertion by the federal government to regulate prices, the flow, the production, and the sale of a provincial national resource.

TEN CENT EXCISE TAX ON GASOLINE   The federal government's ten cent excise tax on gasoline, which was levied to help finance the oil import compensation program, represents another type of federal intrusion in that it restricts the province's own ability to tax this nonrenewable resource.

NATIONAL ENERGY BOARD ACT   —The National Energy Board Act can be seen as challenging the basic principles of provincial resource ownership and management. This act allows the federal government to exercise control of exports (volume and price) of crude oil, natural gas, and related hydrocarbon by-products. Changes in the National Energy Board regulations have been made without provincial input, even though they have had a great impact on the province's and industry's revenues. As such, the provinces of British Columbia, Alberta, and Saskatchewan suggested that increased federal-provincial consultation in these complex jurisdictional matters would help to eliminate some of the existing tensions relating to energy matters.

EMERGENCY SUPPLY ALLOCATION ACT— Western Canada's surplus productive capacity would be of paramount importance in meeting a shortage of supply of crude oil in an emergency. The Task Force felt that there was a lack of provincial representation and input on the Technical Advisory Committee to be set up under this Act. As the owner of the resource, the provinces should be involved in supplying information and in a coordinating role.

FEDERAL GOVERNMENT LEGAL INTERVENTION re: Saskatchewan potash —The federal government has taken an unusual step in directly intervening by legal action against the Province of Saskatchewan in connection with oil and gas royalties and the potash prorationing system. The Task Force was concerned that this represented another type of intrusion into provincial jurisdiction. They agreed that it was a demonstration of a federal challenge to provincial ownership management and development of natural resources.

"CANADA FIRST" POLICY— The stated "Canada First" policy of the federal government with respect to export of nonrenewable resources and the ultimate concept of export control on specific resources (such as coal and uranium) was another area of concern noted by the Task Force. Again, although recognizing the federal government's ultimate control over these matters, they felt that the various provincial responsibilities and needs should be more adequately recognized.

RESOURCE APPRAISAL PROGRAMS— The examples of unilateral federal initiatives in this area considered by the Task Force were the Plains Coal Resource Evaluation Program and the Uranium Reconnaissance Program. It was felt that federal involvement in these areas clouded the general question of resource ownership and jurisdiction. For example, the federal criteria for appraising coal reserves could differ from the provincial criteria that would be used in issuing industrial development permits.

RESEARCH AND DEVELOPMENT PROGRAMS— The federal government has undertaken continuing initiatives in sponsoring research involving provincially-owned resources. This also has the effect of clouding the ownership and management issues related to development of provincial resources.

Past federal research programs have seemed to cover only one aspect of a problem without recognizing the broader development concerns of the provinces. Generally, given these concerns, the Task Force stressed that any federal research initiatives involving provincial resources should take overall provincial objectives into account.

MINERAL POLICY OBJECTIVES—The objective of the federal initiatives in this area is to set standards in regard to resource and export pricing, environmental concerns and manpower objectives. Phases I and II of a Mineral Policy for Canada were implemented in 1972-73 and 1973-74 respectively. Phase III, which now is underway, would give the federal government a greater say in resource development. The Task Force was concerned that this policy could limit the provincial scope of management of mineral resources. As such, they recommended a more careful assessment of the impact of this policy before any further implementation occurred. The concept of resource ownership and resource management by the provinces must also be noted and expanded upon in any mineral policy discussions.

NATIONAL COAL POLICY—   ·The Task Force maintained that since coal is owned by the provinces and is limited to certain geographical areas, any national policy must allow for the participation of the province owning the resource and should take into consideration the legitimate objectives of that province.

In the nonrenewable resource area, the Task Force called for all provinces to reaffirm their constitutional responsibilities, to carefully assess all federal initiatives in light of their own objectives and to demand greater federal-provincial consultation in these areas.

III Housing, Urban Affairs and Land Use

The Task Force was concerned that federal intrusions in these areas could restrict provincial and municipal initiatives, distort provincial and municipal proirities, and strain both federal-provincial and provincial-municipal relations. In many instances, they have either produced or threatened to produce conflicting legislation and regulations between the federal and provincial governments.

Given the extent of provincial jurisdiction in this area, it was felt that these tensions could be eased if the federal government related to local governments through the provincial governments. The Task Force also suggested that the jurisdictions of the federal and provincial governments in these fields be more clearly delineated and that federal-provincial discussions towards this end begin at an early date. Bearing in mind that any grants should go through the provinces, the primary role of the federal government should be to provide loan capital to finance housing and urban development. The primary provincial role should be to formulate housing, urban development and land use policies for the provinces; to deliver all housing programs; and to sponsor experimentation and development of new concepts and processes in housing.

1. Direct Federal Grants to Municipalities

Direct federal grants, such as the Municipal Incentive Grant, may influence provincial policies and priorities. Furthermore, federal actions of this nature in most cases bypass the provincial government. It is, therefore, important that the federal government relate to local government through provincial governments.

2. Housing Programs
[AHOP, Assisted Rental Programs]
These programs directly affect provincial housing policy in a variety of ways: they could change the

balance of owner-occupied to rented housing; they could distort provincial housing markets; and they could counter municipal plans and priorities. These programs also have a great impact on urban land development. The Task Force recommended that greater attention be paid to these results when the proposals are being discussed initially and that better policy coordination between the federal-provincial and the provincial-municipal levels be a priority for all levels of government.

3. Urban Land Development Programs

Federal intrusions in urban land development, through such policies as rail reloctions and urban planning studies, could influence the pattern of urban development, the approval process for land development, the municipal planning process, the timing and location of both industry and urban development, and ultimately, regional development within the province. The Task Force suggested closer liaison between the various federal and provincial agencies with regard to these intrusions.

4. National Guidelines for Land Use Policy

Although this policy has been deferred for the present, the Task Force noted that it could easily be revived and they wanted to reaffirm in the most general sense, that land use is a direct provincial responsibility.

5. Aeronautics Act Amendments

The amendments proposed in Bill C-46, introduced on April 4, 1977, would enable the federal government to control development in the vicinity of airports. Since several provinces already have legislation governing the use of such land, the possibility of conflicting federal and provincial standards and requirements may arise. The Task Force agreed that federal-provincial consultation in this regard is a necessity.

6. Flood Hazard Reduction Program

Concern was expressed that this program might intrude into the provinces' control of land use and development. The federal-provincial program might not complement existing provincial programs that are adequately meeting provincial needs. The Task Force felt that more federal-provincial discussions in this regard would be beneficial.

IV Economic Development

Recent developments within the federal system may be viewed from the perspective of a conscious federal decision to increase its role in the national economic sphere through new policies and increased regulations. Corresponding to such moves has been a growing, adverse feeling in the west regarding the federal government's lack of understanding of regional needs and objectives as well as its tendency to bias economic decisions towards the aspirations of central Canada. Both the federal and provincial governments have legitimate responsibilities within the field of economic development. On various fronts, federal actions seriously affect the direction of provincial development. In general, federal intrusions in the economic development field take the form of federal actions which limit the scope for independent provincial programs and policies.

The Task Force recommended that there be an increased coordination of effort between the federal government and the western provinces to develop viable agricultural and industrial development strategies for western Canada. More provincial input into national economic decision-making is needed. This could be undertaken in a variety of ways and in a number of areas.

1. Agriculture

INCOME STABILIZATION ACTS—Although these acts are relatively recent enactments, their administration and responsiveness to changing market situations could be improved. As well, there should be harmonization of federal and provincial programs on a national basis. For example, the federal government's delay in rectifying the situation surrounding the cow/calf program meant that many of the provinces developed their own programs and that some problems now exist in harmonizing the previous provincial programs with the national one.

CREDIT— Farm Credit Corporation loans were severely restricted as a result of a 1975 federal budget cutback. The resulting decrease in available credit has tended to discourage the family farm and to increase the financial pressure on local and provincial lending institutions. The Task Force felt that this was yet another example which pointed out the need for improved federal-provincial cooperation in order to obtain the objective of balanced growth in agriculture.

FEDERAL LEVY ON FLUID MILK— Concern was expressed about certain aspecs of the federal government's recently announced dairy policy for 1977-78. The federal government's proposal for placing a levy on fluid milk is an intrusion into a market that traditionally has been under provincial pricing jurisdiction. The Task Force recommended that the federal government reassess this proposed policy in light of these concerns.

2. Transportation

The Task Force agreed that the deficiencies in the transportation infrastructure serving the region are a major obstacle to a faster and more balanced rate of economic development in the west. The Task Force did not question the federal government's jurisdiction in the interprovincial transportation field, but rather the manner in which the authority was exercised. They felt that the federal government has tended to view transportation policy in its narrowest sense. An example of this tendency can be found in the federal proposal to set freight rates according to "what traffic will bear". The Task Force reaffirmed that transportation is fundamental to the achievement of diversification of the economic base in the western provinces. They asked that the federal government develop a more equitable transportation system to meet the economic objectives of the western provinces.

3. Trade [GATT]

Although the federal government's responsibility for negotiating international trade agreements is clear and is therefore not an "intrusion", the Task Force viewed provincial input into the final position on international trade negotiations to be of utmost importance, given the significance of foreign market objectives. The liberalization of trade with the reduction of trade barriers is vital to the development in the west of a secure economic base; to aid industries reliant on natural growth through secondary industry; and to develop a strong manufacturing sector. As a result, the Task Force called for a more active and substantial role for the provinces in the formulation of national policies in such areas as GATT negotiations.

4. Industrial Development

The Task Force expressed concern that many of the federal government's recent industrial development strategies ignored regional aspirations and disregarded the concept of upgrading near the source of raw materials. With regard to the Federal Throne Speech announcements of upcoming aid to small businesses, it was felt that this federal proposal was commendable but that care should be taken to ensure that the policies developed are complementary to the aspirations of the provinces.

5. Environmental Concerns

Recent federal initiatives in the area of pollution control regulations have caused some duplication and have implications for resource ownership. Federal environmental studies are another area of concern since they may result in recommendations affecting provincial land use, water use, and development programs with little regard for specific provincial needs. With regard to environmental matters, the Task Force recommended that priority be given to provincial objectives and suggested that in many instances federal minimum standards with provincial responsibility for application and enforcement would resolve most conflicts.

6. DREE

The potential for a conflict between DREE activities and provincial priorities exists. With this in mind, the Task Force agreed that there must be recognition that the provincial governments retain primary responsibility for establishing the priorities for economic development. All DREE sub-agreements should reflect provincial priorities. To ensure compatibility with provincial objectives, priority should be given to sharing of existing or planned provincial programs rather than the creation of new programs to suit DREE involvement.

V Communications

Recent federal actions, in the field of communications, have tended to expand federal control over those aspects which are entirely local and intra-provincial in nature, such as closed circuit cable and educational television, provincial laws relating to commercial advertising, and cable distribution systems. The Task Force felt that some aspects of communications policy should be subject to provincial control and jurisdiction and frequently shared common concerns with respect to these federal intrusions in the communications policy field.

The Task Force made the following comments and recommendations:

1. Telecommunications

CABLE TELEVISION— The federal government, through the extension of its authority under the Broadcasting Act, has proposed a policy toward pay television which will involve federal regulation of closed circuit entertainment services provided by coaxial cable. Recent actions taken by the Canadian Radio-Television and Telecommunications Commission (CRTC) regulating Master Antenna Television Systems and Cable television licensing have also expanded federal control over cable communication systems. The provinces of Alberta, Saskatchewan, and Manitoba recommended that cable services which do not directly involve the relay, re-transmission or amplificiation of broadcast signals be clearly subject to provincial control. Undertakings which offer these non-broadcast services should be required to submit to the province regulations insofar as these services are concerned. The province of British Columbia was sympathetic to this view.

CABLE DISTRIBUTION SYSTEMS— The provinces of Alberta and Saskatchewan recommended that cable distribution systems, being local works or undertakings, should be subject to provincial law, in accordance with Section 92 (10) of the British North America Act. They also agreed that control and regulation of cable distribution systems should revert to the provinces; and that the federal government should continue to regulate these systems only in relation to their use within the Canadian broadcasting system.

2. Educational and Cultural Communications

The federal government's attempts to impose a definition of "programming" on the provinces would restrict a provincial government's use of communications technologies to deliver social, educational and cultural services to the public. The provinces of Alberta and Saskatchewan agreed that educational communications carried out by means of cable or wire technology should be exclusively a provincial concern. British Columbia was sympathetic to this position. Manitoba had already satisfactorily resolved this issue with the federal government through their agreement on programming and carrier ownership.

3. Commercial Advertising Regulation

The CRTC's steps to regulate commercial television advertising will affect the validity and scope of provincial laws relating to advertising. The provinces of British Columbia and Saskatchewan agreed that the commercial content of advertisements used by broadcast undertakings should be subject to provincial laws relating to advertising. They recommend that formal delegation of this responsibility to the appropriate federal regulatory agency responsible for the implementation of provincial laws vis-a-vis broadcast licensees be considered, provided the federal government enters into bilateral arrangements in this regard.

4. Federal Interconnection Policies

The federal government's interconnection policies favour a liberalization of rules, which permit the connection of customer-owned terminal attachments and interconnection between the networks of federally-regulated carriers. The provinces of Alberta and Saskatchewan recommend the provinces continue to oppose any federal moves encouraging these actions, which would diminish the provinces' control over their telecommunications carriers, and which result in a deterioration of levels of service to remote and rural areas. British Columbia was sympathetic to these views. ....

INDEX

Printed in USA